Become a top fact-fetcher with CGP!

Quick question — do you own CGP's
Knowledge Organiser for AQA GCSE Physics?

You do? Great! Now you can use this Knowledge Retriever
to check you've really remembered all the crucial facts.

There are two memory tests for each topic, plus mixed quiz questions
to make extra sure it's all stuck in your brain. Enjoy.

CGP — still the best! ☺

Our sole aim here at CGP is to produce the highest quality books —
carefully written, immaculately presented and dangerously close to being funny.

Then we work our socks off to get them out to you
— at the cheapest possible prices.

Contents

How to Use This Book............................2

Working Scientifically
The Scientific Method............................3
Designing & Performing Experiments............5
Presenting Data............................7
Conclusions, Evaluations and Units............9
Mixed Practice Quizzes............................11

Topic 1 — Energy
Energy Stores, Transfers and Systems............13
Energy, Power and Efficiency............15
Reducing Unwanted Energy Transfers............17
Non-Renewables and Renewables............19
Renewables............................21
Renewables and Trends............23
Mixed Practice Quizzes............25

Topic 2 — Electricity
Current............................27
$V = IR$ and Circuit Symbols............29
I-V Characteristics & Circuit Devices............31
Series and Parallel Circuits............33
Mixed Practice Quizzes............35
Electricity in the Home............37
Energy, Power and the National Grid............39
Static Electricity............................41
Electric Fields............................43
Mixed Practice Quizzes............45

Topic 3 — Particle Model of Matter
Density, States and Internal Energy............47
Heating and Cooling............................49
Particle Motion in Gases............51
Mixed Practice Quizzes............53

Topic 4 — Atomic Structure
Developing the Model of the Atom............55
Isotopes and Nuclear Radiation............57
Radioactivity and Risk............................59
Background Radiation and Uses............61
Mixed Practice Quizzes............63

Topic 5 — Forces
Scalars, Vectors, Forces and Weight............65
Calculating Forces and Work Done............67
Mixed Practice Quizzes............69
Forces and Elasticity............................71
Moments............................73
Fluid Pressure and Upthrust............75
Mixed Practice Quizzes............77
Motion............................79
Distance-Time & Velocity-Time Graphs............81
Newton's Laws of Motion............83
Mixed Practice Quizzes............85
Terminal Velocity and Reaction Times............87
Stopping Distances............................89
Momentum............................91
Mixed Practice Quizzes............93

Topic 6 — Waves

Transverse and Longitudinal Waves..............95
Speed of Sound and Reflection..........................97
Refraction and EM Waves..............................99
Uses and Dangers of EM Waves..............101
Mixed Practice Quizzes..................................103
Lenses and Magnification................................105
Ray Diagrams..107
Visible Light..109
Mixed Practice Quizzes....................................111
Emitting and Absorbing Radiation................113
Sound Waves..115
Uses of Sound Waves....................................117
Mixed Practice Quizzes....................................119

Topic 7 — Magnetism and Electromagnetism

Magnets..121
Compasses and Electromagnetism................123
The Motor Effect..125
The Generator Effect and Microphones....127
Generators and Transformers..........................129
Mixed Practice Quizzes....................................131

Topic 8 — Space Physics

Stars and the Solar System..................................133
Orbits, Red-Shift and The Big Bang..........135
Mixed Practice Quizzes....................................137

Required Practicals

Required Practicals 1..139
Required Practicals 2..141
Required Practicals 3..143
Required Practicals 4..145
Required Practicals 5..147
Required Practicals 6..149
Mixed Practice Quizzes....................................151

Practical Skills

Apparatus and Techniques..............................153
Working with Electronics..............................155
Mixed Practice Quizzes....................................157

Published by CGP.
From original material by Richard Parsons.
Editors: Laura Collins, Georgina Fairclough, Mary Falkner, Emily Garrett, Duncan Lindsay and Luke Molloy.
Contributor: Paddy Gannon.

With thanks to Glenn Rogers for the proofreading.
With thanks to Emily Smith for the copyright research.

ISBN: 978 1 78908 495 5

Data used to construct stopping distance graph on pages 89 and 90 from the Highway Code.
Contains public sector information licensed under the Open Government Licence v3.0.
http://www.nationalarchives.gov.uk/doc/open-government-licence/version/3/

Printed by Elanders Ltd, Newcastle upon Tyne.
Clipart from Corel®
Illustrations by: Sandy Gardner Artist, email sandy@sandygardner.co.uk

How to Use This Book

Every page in this book has a matching page in the GCSE Physics **Knowledge Organiser**.
Before using this book, try to **memorise** everything on a Knowledge Organiser page.
Then follow these **seven steps** to see how much knowledge you're able to retrieve...

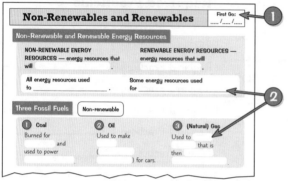

1 In this book, there are two versions of each page. Find the **'First Go'** of the page you've tried to memorise, and write the **date** at the top.

2 Use what you've learned from the Knowledge Organiser to **fill in** any dotted lines or white spaces.

⎨ You may need to draw, complete or add labels to diagrams too. ⎬

3 Use the Knowledge Organiser to **check your work**.
Use a **different colour pen** to write in anything you missed or that wasn't quite right.
This lets you see clearly what you **know** and what you **don't know**.

4 After doing the First Go page, **wait a few days**. This is important because **spacing out** your retrieval practice helps you to remember things better.

5 Now do the **Second Go** page.
⎨ The Second Go page is harder — it has more things missing. ⎬

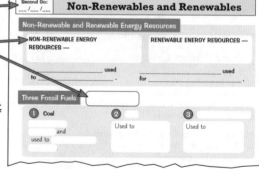

6 Again, check your work against the Knowledge Organiser and **correct it** with a different colour pen.
You should see some **improvement** between your first and second go.

7 **Wait** another few days, then try recreating the whole Knowledge Organiser page on a **blank piece of paper**. If you can do this, you'll know you've **really learned it**.

There are also **Mixed Practice Quizzes** dotted throughout the book:
• The quizzes come in sets of four. They test a mix of content from the previous few pages.
• Do each quiz on a different day — write the date you do each one at the top of the quiz.
• Tick the questions you get right and record your score in the box at the end.

The Scientific Method

First Go:
..... /..... /.....

Developing Theories

Come up with [_____]

⬇

[_____]

⬇

Evidence is peer-reviewed

⬇

If all evidence backs up [_____], it becomes an [_____].

HYPOTHESIS — a possible [_____].

PEER REVIEW — when other scientists check results and explanations before [_____].

[_____] can still change over time.

e.g. the theory of atomic structure:

Models

REPRESENTATIONAL MODELS — a simplified [_____] or picture of the [_____], e.g. the molecular model of matter:

Models help scientists explain [_____] and make [_____].

COMPUTATIONAL MODELS — [_____] are used to simulate [_____].

Issues in Science

Scientific developments can create four issues:

1 Economic — e.g. beneficial technology, like alternative energy sources, may be [_____].

2 Environmental — e.g. [_____] could [____] the natural environment.

3 Social — Decisions based on [_____] can affect people, e.g. [_____] fossil fuels.

4 Personal — some decisions affect [_____], e.g. a person may not want a wind farm being built [_____].

Media reports on scientific developments may be [_____], [_____] or biased.

Hazard and Risk

HAZARD — something that could potentially [_____].

RISK — the chance that a [_____].

Hazards associated with physics experiments include:

• [_____] from lasers.

• Faulty [_____] equipment.

• Fire from [_____].

The seriousness of the [_____] and the likelihood of [_____] both need consideration.

 ✓ ✓ ✓

The Scientific Method

Developing Theories

_____

⬇

_____

Evidence is _____

⬇

If all _____

HYPOTHESIS — _____

PEER REVIEW — _____

_____ can still change over time _____.

e.g. _____:

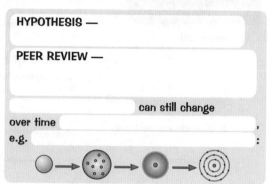

Models

REPRESENTATIONAL MODELS — _____

_____, e.g. the molecular model _____:

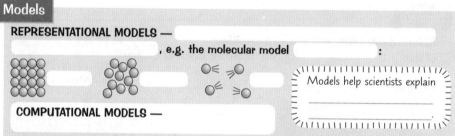

COMPUTATIONAL MODELS — _____

Models help scientists explain
_____
_____.

Issues in Science

Scientific developments can create four issues:

1 Economic —

2 Environmental —

3 Social —

4 Personal —

_____ on scientific developments may be _____.

Hazard and Risk

HAZARD — _____

RISK — _____

Hazards associated with physics experiments include:

• _____

• Faulty _____.

• _____

The seriousness of _____
_____
_____

Designing & Performing Experiments

Collecting Data

	Data should be...
REPEATABLE	Same person gets same results after _____ using the _____ method and equipment.
REPRODUCIBLE	Similar results can be achieved by _____, or by using a different method or piece of _____.
ACCURATE	Results are close to the _____.
PRECISE	All data is close to _____.

Reliable data is _____ and _____.

↓

Valid results are _____ and _____ and answer the _____.

Fair Tests

INDEPENDENT VARIABLE	Variable that you _____.
DEPENDENT VARIABLE	Variable that _____.
CONTROL VARIABLE	Variable that is _____.
CONTROL EXPERIMENT	An experiment kept under _____ as _____ without anything being done to it.
FAIR TEST	An experiment where only _____ changes, whilst all other variables are _____.

_____ _____ are carried out when variables can't be controlled.

Four Things to Look Out For

1. **RANDOM ERRORS —** _____ caused by things like _____ in measuring.
2. **SYSTEMATIC ERRORS —** measurements that are wrong by _____
3. **ZERO ERRORS —** systematic errors that are caused by using _____ that isn't _____.
4. **ANOMALOUS RESULTS —** results that _____ with the rest of the data.

Anomalous results can be _____ if you know what _____.

Processing Data

Calculate the _____ — add together all data values and _____.

UNCERTAINTY — the amount by which a _____ may differ from the _____.

$$\text{uncertainty} = \frac{\text{_____}}{\text{_____ minus _____}}$$

In any calculation, you should round the answer to the _____ number of significant figures (s.f.) given.

Working Scientifically

Designing & Performing Experiments

Collecting Data

	Data should be...	
REPRODUCIBLE		**Valid results are**
	All data	

Fair Tests

.... can't be controlled.

DEPENDENT VARIABLE —

— an experiment kept

Four Things to Look Out For

1 **RANDOM ERRORS —**

2 **SYSTEMATIC ERRORS —**

3 **ZERO ERRORS —**

4 **ANOMALOUS RESULTS —**

Anomalous results ....
....

In any calculation, ...
....

Processing Data

— add together

UNCERTAINTY —

$$uncertainty = \frac{\rule{1cm}{0.4pt}}{\rule{0.5cm}{0.4pt}}$$

Presenting Data

Bar Charts

Bar charts are used when independent variable is [   ] or [   ].

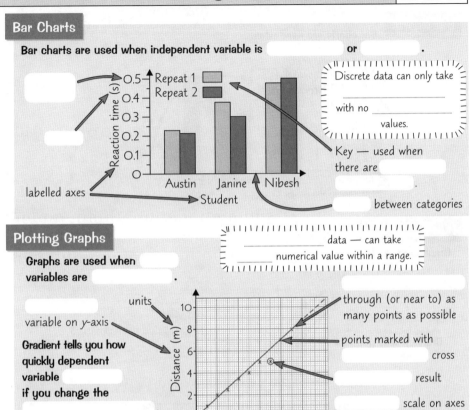

Discrete data can only take
....
with no ....
values.

Key — used when there are [   ].

labelled axes

Repeat 1
Repeat 2

Austin   Janine   Nibesh
Student

[   ] between categories

Plotting Graphs

Graphs are used when [   ] variables are [   ].

....
.... data — can take
.... numerical value within a range.

units

[   ] variable on y-axis

Gradient tells you how quickly dependent variable [   ] if you change the [   ].

gradient = ——————————

through (or near to) as many points as possible

points marked with [   ] cross

[   ] result

[   ] scale on axes

[   ] variable on x-axis

Three Types of Correlation Between Variables

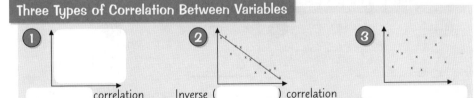

[   ] correlation   Inverse ([   ]) correlation   [   ]

Possible reasons for a correlation:

Chance — correlation might be [   ].

Third variable — [   ] the two variables.

Cause — if every other variable that could affect the result is [   ], you can conclude that changing one variable [   ].

 ☑   ☑   ☑

Working Scientifically

8

Presenting Data

Bar Charts

Bar charts are used when _____

_____ .

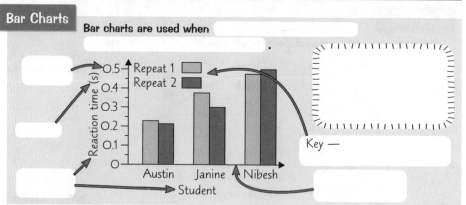

Key —

Plotting Graphs

Graphs are used _____

_____ — can take _____ .

Gradient tells you how

points marked

gradient = ————————————

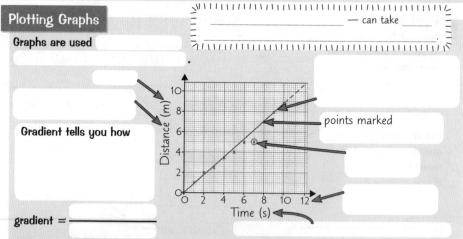

Three Types of Correlation Between Variables

1   2   3

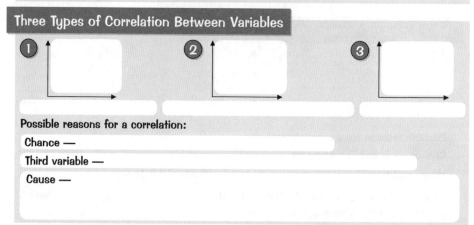

Possible reasons for a correlation:

Chance —

Third variable —

Cause —

 ✓ ✓ ✓

Conclusions, Evaluations and Units

First Go:
..... /..... /.....

Conclusions

Draw conclusion by [_____] between [_____] variables.

You can only draw a conclusion from [_____] — you can't go any further than that.

Justify conclusion using [_____].

Refer to [_____] and state whether [_____].

Evaluations

EVALUATION — a [_____] of the whole investigation.

	Things to consider
Method	• Validity of [_____] • [_____] variables
Results	• Reliability, [_____], [_____] and [_____] of results • Number of [_____] • Level of [_____] in the results
Anomalous results	• Causes of any [_____] results

You could make [_____] based on your conclusion, which you could test [_____].

Repeating experiment with changes to improve the [_____] will give you more [_____] in your conclusions.

S.I. Units

S.I. BASE UNITS — a set of [_____] that [_____] use.

Quantity	S.I. Unit
	kilogram ( )
length	[____] ( )
	second ( )
temperature	[____] ( )

Scaling Units

SCALING PREFIX — a word or symbol that goes before [_____] to indicate a [_____].

Multiple of unit	Prefix
	tera ( )
10^9	( )
	(M)
1000	( )
	deci ( )
0.01	( )
	(m)
10^{-6}	( )
	nano ( )

kg ⇄ g

m^3 ⇄ cm^3

kg/m^3 ⇄ g/cm^3

Working Scientifically

Conclusions, Evaluations and Units

Conclusions

Draw conclusion by

⬇

.

⬇

Refer to

.

You can only draw a conclusion from

.... — you can't

....

....

Evaluations

EVALUATION —

.

You could ....

....

based on your conclusion,

....

....

	Things to consider
Method	•
	•
	•
	•
	•
Anomalous results	•

Repeating experiment

S.I. Units

S.I. BASE UNITS — ....

....

....

....

Quantity	S.I. Unit
	second (........)

Scaling Units

SCALING PREFIX —

Multiple of unit	Prefix
	tera (........)
10^{-6}	

kg ⇄

⇄

⇄ g/cm³

Mixed Practice Quizzes

Hazard: Quiz questions testing pages 3-10. Risk of doing them: Falling asleep.
Risk of ignoring them: Struggling with science. Conclusion: Give them a try.

Quiz 1   Date: ...... / ...... / ......

1) How do you calculate the range of a set of data?

2) What does it mean if results are valid?

3) Give an example of a personal problem
   that scientific development can cause.

4) State one hazard that is associated with physics experiments.

5) True or false? Accurate results are results that are close to the mean.

6) What is meant by the 'evaluation' of an investigation?

7) What do you have to divide by to get from cm^3 to m^3?

8) State one suitable way to present data
   when the independent variable is discrete.

9) What is an anomalous result?

10) What equation can be used to find the gradient of a graph?

Total:

Quiz 2   Date: ...... / ...... / ......

1) Describe how a hypothesis can become an accepted theory.

2) What is a 'dependent variable'?

3) Give two reasons why a correlation may arise between two variables,
   even if changing one variable doesn't cause the other to change.

4) Give one example of an accepted theory that has changed over time.

5) When can an anomalous result in a data set be ignored?

6) Give the equation used to find the uncertainty for a set of values.

7) State three things that should be considered when evaluating results.

8) True or false? The metre (m) is an S.I. unit used to measure length.

9) Define the term 'peer review'.

10) What is a hazard?

Total:

Mixed Practice Quizzes

Quiz 3   Date: ...... / ...... / ......

1) What is a representational model?
2) Which variable goes on the x-axis of a graph?
3) Describe how to write up a conclusion to an experiment.
4) Define each of the following terms:
   a) Independent variable
   b) Control variable
5) Name two types of experimental error.
6) Which term describes a possible explanation for an observation?
7) What is meant by the term 'uncertainty' when describing data?
8) Which scaling prefix indicates a multiplying factor of 10^6?
9) What does a graph of data with a positive correlation look like?
10) Give one issue associated with media
    reports on scientific developments.

Total:

Quiz 4   Date: ...... / ...... / ......

1) What is: a) repeatable data? b) reproducible data?
2) Give a suitable way to represent data when both variables are continuous.
3) State the S.I. unit for temperature.
4) Give four types of issue that can result from scientific developments.
5) When is a key used in a bar chart?
6) Describe how to calculate the mean of a set of values.
7) True or false? A conclusion cannot go beyond what the data shows.
8) What multiple is nano (n) a prefix for?
9) Give two types of correlation that may arise from a graph.
10) Give two ways in which models can be useful to scientists.

Total:

Energy Stores, Transfers and Systems

Eight Types of Energy Store

1. _____
2. _____ potential
3. _____ potential
4. Electrostatic
5. _____
6. Chemical
7. Magnetic
8. _____

Four Types of Energy Transfer

1. _____ (a force doing work)
2. Electrical (_____)
3. _____
4. Radiation (e.g. _____)

_____ = energy transferred.

Energy Transfers in Five Different Systems

SYSTEM — a single object or ....

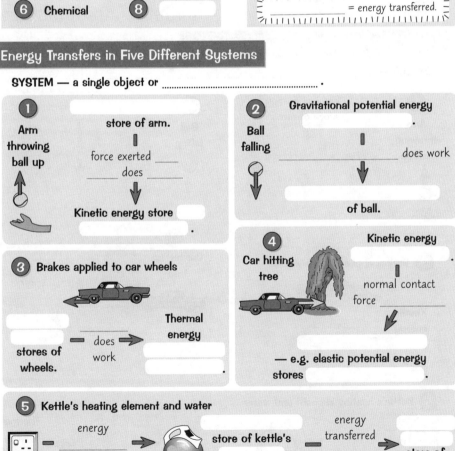

1. _____
   Arm throwing ball up
   _____ store of arm.
   force exerted ____ does ____
   Kinetic energy store _____ .

2. Gravitational potential energy
   _____ .
   Ball falling
   _____ does work
   _____ of ball.

3. Brakes applied to car wheels
   _____ stores of wheels.
   — does work →
   Thermal energy _____ .

4. Car hitting tree
   Kinetic energy _____ .
   normal contact force _____
   — e.g. elastic potential energy stores _____ .

5. Kettle's heating element and water
   _____ energy _____
   → _____ store of kettle's _____ element.
   energy transferred _____
   → _____ store of water.

 ✓   ✓   ✓

Energy Stores, Transfers and Systems

Eight Types of Energy Store

1.
2.
3.
4.
5.   7.
6.   8.

Four Types of Energy Transfer

1.
2.
3.
4.

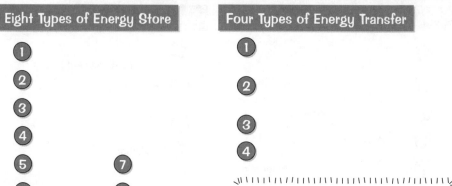

=

Energy Transfers in Five Different Systems

SYSTEM — ....

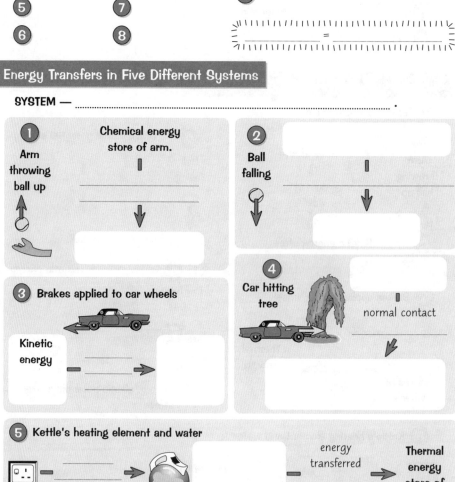

1. Arm throwing ball up

Chemical energy store of arm.

2. Ball falling

3. Brakes applied to car wheels

Kinetic energy

4. Car hitting tree

normal contact

5. Kettle's heating element and water

energy transferred

Thermal energy store of water.

Energy, Power and Efficiency

Kinetic Energy

Kinetic energy ( )

$$E_k = \tfrac{1}{2}m\quad^2$$

(kg)   speed ( )

Gravitational Potential Energy

(kg)

(J) $E_p = mgh$ (m)

gravitational ( )

Conservation of Energy and Specific Heat Capacity

CONSERVATION OF ENERGY — energy can be _____,
_____ or _____ but not _____ or _____.

Energy _____
(by heating) _____

_____, increasing its _____

_____.

Some _____
as energy transferred to
_____
of surroundings.

SPECIFIC HEAT CAPACITY — ....
....

CLOSED SYSTEM — no _____
_____ is transferred _____
_____, so there is
_____ in total energy.

In _____, energy is
_____ (wasted) to a store that's
_____ (usually thermal).

Power

POWER — _____
(or rate of doing work).
One watt (W) = one _____ of energy
_____. (J)

energy transferred ( )

$$P = \frac{E}{t}$$

power ( )   _____ (s)

$$P = \frac{}{t}$$

power ( )   _____ (s)

2 W motor transfers
_____
_____ than 1 W
motor, so lifts mass faster.

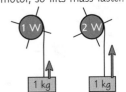

Efficiency Equations

energy transfer

$$\text{Efficiency} = \frac{}{\text{Total input}\ }$$

$$\text{Efficiency} = \frac{}{\text{Total power input}}$$

No device is _____.

Multiply by _____
to get _____.

Energy, Power and Efficiency

Kinetic Energy

$$E_k = \tfrac{1}{2}mv^2$$

Gravitational Potential Energy

height (m)

$$E_p =$$

Conservation of Energy and Specific Heat Capacity

CONSERVATION OF ENERGY —

Energy

Some energy dissipated

SPECIFIC HEAT CAPACITY —

CLOSED SYSTEM —

In _____, energy is _____ to a store that's _____

Power

POWER —

One watt (W) =

_____ than 1 W
motor _____

$$P = \frac{}{\text{time (s)}}$$

$$P = \frac{}{\text{time (s)}}$$

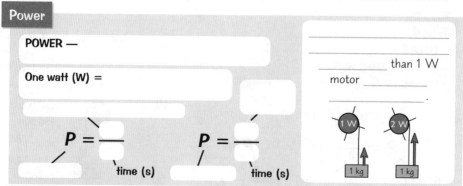

Efficiency Equations

Efficiency = —————

Efficiency = —————

Multiply by _____

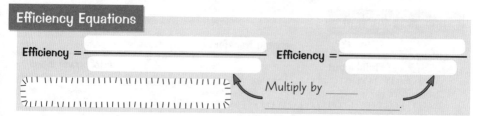

Reducing Unwanted Energy Transfers

Conduction

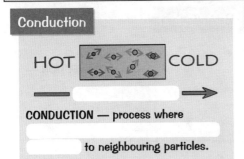

HOT ————— COLD

CONDUCTION — process where

_____ to neighbouring particles.

Convection

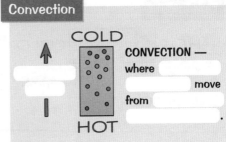

COLD

CONVECTION — where _____ move from _____ .

HOT

Lubrication and Thermal Insulation

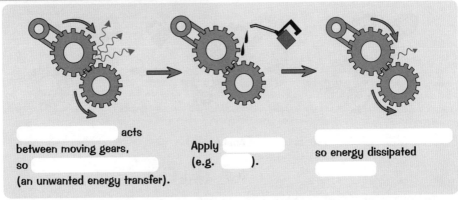

_____ acts between moving gears, so _____ (an unwanted energy transfer).

Apply _____ (e.g. _____).

so energy dissipated _____

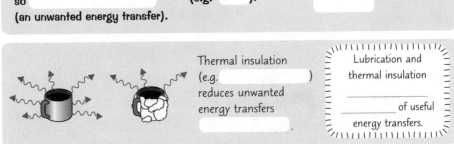

Thermal insulation (e.g. _____) reduces unwanted energy transfers _____ .

Lubrication and thermal insulation _____ _____ of useful energy transfers.

Two Ways to Decrease How Quickly a Building Cools

1. Increase _____ of its _____ .

2. Make walls out of material with _____ .

The higher a material's ....,' the .... it transfers energy by ....

18

| Second Go: ..... /..... /..... | **Reducing Unwanted Energy Transfers** |

Conduction

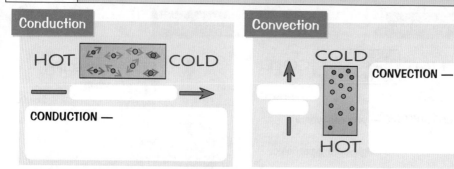

HOT   COLD

CONDUCTION —

Convection

COLD

CONVECTION —

HOT

Lubrication and Thermal Insulation

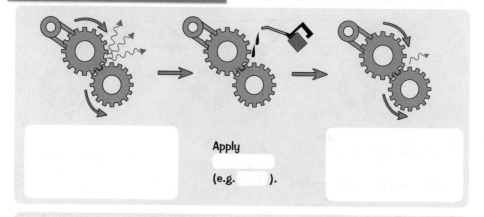

Apply

(e.g.   ).

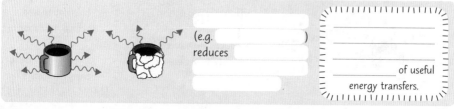

(e.g.)
reduces

.... of useful
energy transfers.

Two Ways to Decrease How Quickly a Building Cools

1️⃣   —   The higher

2️⃣ Make walls   .

Non-Renewables and Renewables

Non-Renewable and Renewable Energy Resources

NON-RENEWABLE ENERGY RESOURCES — energy resources that will _____ .

RENEWABLE ENERGY RESOURCES — energy resources that will _____ .

All energy resources used to ....

Some energy resources used for ....

Three Fossil Fuels   Non-renewable

1 Coal
Burned for _____ and used to power _____ .

2 Oil
Used to make _____ (_____) for cars.

3 (Natural) Gas
Used to _____ that is then _____ .

Fossil fuels are _____ .
- Burning fossil fuels _____ , contributing to _____ .
- Burning coal and oil releases _____ , causing _____ .

Reliable

Nuclear Power _____

Nuclear fuel _____ in nuclear _____ , _____

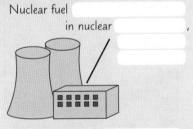

- Nuclear waste is _____ to _____ .
- Carries the risk of a _____

Wind Power   Renewable

Wind turns .... , generating ....

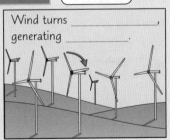

- Produce _____ when in use.
- _____
- _____

Unreliable — Turbines stop turning when ....

Second Go:
...../...../.....

Non-Renewables and Renewables

Non-Renewable and Renewable Energy Resources

NON-RENEWABLE ENERGY
RESOURCES —

RENEWABLE ENERGY RESOURCES —

.... used
to ....

.... used
for ....

Three Fossil Fuels

1 Coal

and
used to

2

Used to

3

Used to

Fossil fuels are ....
- **Burning**
- **Burning**

Nuclear Power

Nuclear

- **Nuclear waste**

- **Carries the risk**

Wind Power

Wind ....
....

-
-
-

Unreliable — ....
....

 ✓ ✓ ✓

Renewables

Solar Power

Solar cells ....
directly from ....
....

- **Produce** [........................]
  when in use.

Reliable (........................)
....

```
........................ use the
sun to ........................ which is
then pumped into ........................ .
```

Geothermal Power

power plant

water

hot rock

Energy from .... of
underground hot rocks
used to ....
....

- **Do very little** [........................]
  .

[........................]   [........................ are used to ....]

Hydro-electric Power   [Renewable]

.... , built in
valley, ...

Water allowed out ....
.... , generating electricity.

- **Produce** [........................]
  when in use.
- [........................] (from
  flooding the valley) release
  [........................] ,
  contributing to global warming.

Reliable (except ....
........................).

Wave Power   [Renewable]

air

Waves move [........] → **Air forced** [........] → [........]

- **Produce** [........] when in use.
- **Disturb habitats of** [........]
- [........]

Unreliable — ....
....

Renewables

Second Go:
..... /..... /.....

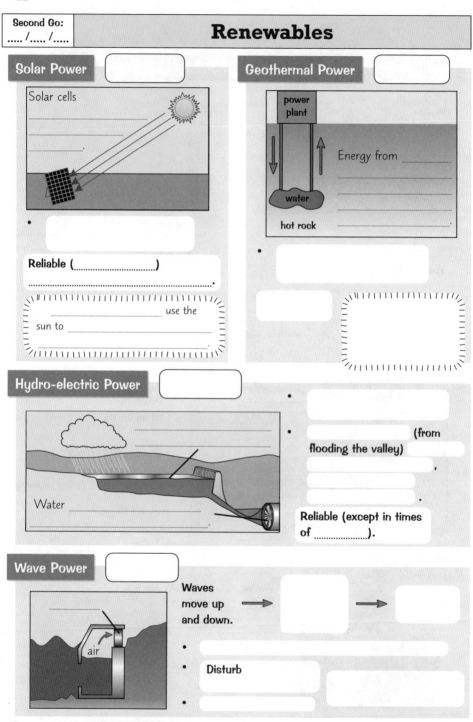

Solar Power

Solar cells

....

....

....

•

Reliable (.................................)

....

.... use the
sun to ....
....

Geothermal Power

power plant

Energy from ....
....
....
....

•

Hydro-electric Power

....

Water ....
....

•

• .... (from flooding the valley)

,

.

Reliable (except in times of ....).

Wave Power

air

Waves move up and down. →

→

•

• Disturb

•

Topic 1 — Energy

Renewables and Trends

Tidal Barrages

Renewable

Tide comes in.

↓

Water builds

_____

_____ .

↓

Water _____
_____ .

→ _____

- Produce _____ when in use.
- Disturb habitats of _____ .
- _____ .

Reliable — ....
....

_____ built across
_____

Bio-fuels

Made from _____
or _____ .

Bio-fuels are burned to _____
.

- In some regions,
_____

_____ destroyed to

_____ ,

so species lose

_____ .

Reliable

Bio-fuels are also _____
_____ and used
as _____ .

Trends in Energy Use

1900
– 2000 ⟹ Electricity use increased as:
- _____ and people began to use
_____ .

2000
onwards ⟹ Electricity use decreasing as:
- appliances are _____ .
- people are _____ with amount of _____ .

Three reasons why we're increasing use of renewables:

1 _____ is very damaging to environment.

2 We need to _____
_____ without _____
before they run out.

3 Pressure on _____
have led them to _____

_____

_____ .

Scientists can advise others to use _____ , but don't
have the power to _____ . Change limited by _____
_____

Second Go:
..... / ..... / .....

Renewables and Trends

Tidal Barrages

Tide comes in.

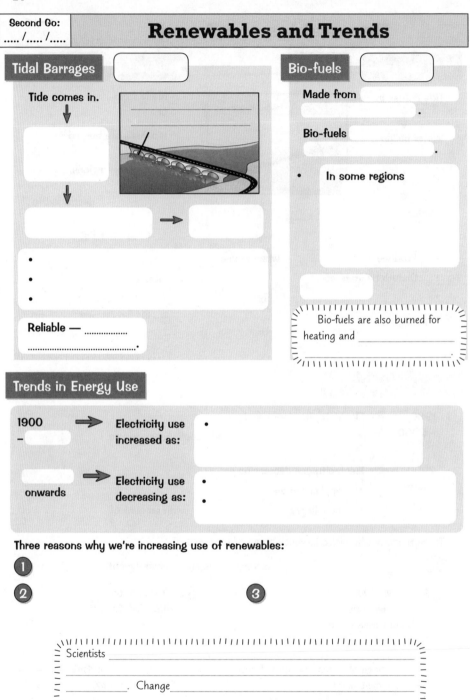

-
-
-

Reliable — ....
....

Bio-fuels

Made from

.

Bio-fuels

.

- In some regions

Bio-fuels are also burned for heating and _____

Trends in Energy Use

1900 → Electricity use increased as:
–

-

onwards → Electricity use decreasing as:

-
-

Three reasons why we're increasing use of renewables:

1

2   **3**

Scientists _____

_____ . Change _____

Mixed Practice Quizzes

If you think doing quizzes based on stuff from pages 13-24 sounds like a bad idea, don't look down. Oh no, you looked. That means you have to do them now.

Quiz 1   Date: ...... / ...... / ......

1) State two environmental impacts of burning fossil fuels.
2) In what type of system is there no overall change in energy when energy is transferred?
3) Would a building cool quicker with thinner or thicker walls?
4) Give one reason why electricity use increased from 1900 to 2000.
5) Name three types of energy stores.
6) True or false? In some systems, energy is never dissipated.
7) What is one joule of energy per second in watts?
8) Give two equations that can be used to calculate power.
9) What are bio-fuels made from?
10) Describe how energy is transferred when a car hits a tree.

Total:

Quiz 2   Date: ...... / ...... / ......

1) True or false? Energy can be transferred usefully, created or destroyed.
2) Which one of the following is a non-renewable energy resource?
   A. Wind power   B. Bio-fuels   C. Tidal power   D. Nuclear power
3) Describe how energy is transferred when a kettle boils water.
4) What is meant by the specific heat capacity of a substance?
5) Which is more reliable, wave power or solar power?
6) Give two reasons why the use of renewable energy resources is increasing.
7) What equation can be used to find the amount of energy in an object's kinetic energy store?
8) Name three renewable energy resources.
9) State two negative impacts tidal barrages have on the environment.
10) True or false? Thermal insulation can increase the efficiency of useful energy transfers.

Total:

Topic 1 — Energy

Mixed Practice Quizzes

Quiz 3   Date: ...... / ...... / ......

1) True or false? The higher a material's thermal conductivity,
   the faster it transfers energy by conduction.

2) Name three types of fossil fuel. Give one use for each type of fossil fuel.

3) Describe one environmental impact of using nuclear power.

4) Does thermal insulation increase or decrease unwanted energy transfers?

5) What equation can be used to find the amount of energy in an object's
   gravitational potential energy store?

6) Scientists can advise others to change from non-renewable to renewable
   energy resources, but what factors is this change limited by?

7) What type of energy store is dissipated energy usually transferred to?

8) What is meant by a renewable energy resource?

9) True or false? Energy can be transferred magnetically.

10) Explain why tidal power is more reliable than wave power.

Total:

Quiz 4   Date: ...... / ...... / ......

1) What is meant by a system?

2) Describe one environmental impact of using hydro-electric power.

3) What is meant by the conservation of energy?

4) Give two equations that can be used to calculate efficiency.

5) Explain how using lubrication on moving gears can reduce the energy
   they dissipate.

6) State two negative impacts wind turbines have on the environment.

7) Name an energy resource that doesn't produce pollution when in use.

8) True or false? A 2 W motor would lift a 1 kg mass faster than a 1 W motor.

9) Describe the changes in the way energy is stored when:
   a) a ball is thrown upwards   b) a ball falls under gravity

10) Energy resources can be used to generate electricity.
    State two other uses of energy resources.

Total:

Current

Current, Potential Difference and Resistance

	Definition	Unit
CURRENT	flow of	........................, A
POTENTIAL DIFFERENCE	.... that pushes charge round	volt, ...
RESISTANCE	anything that .... charge flow	ohm, ...

Current in Circuits

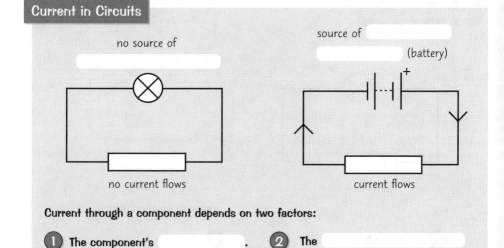

no source of

[   ]

no current flows

source of [   ]

[   ] (battery)

current flows

Current through a component depends on two factors:

1 The component's [   ].

The greater the [   ],

the [   ] the current.

2 The [   ]

[   ] the component.

The greater the [   ]

[   ], the [   ]

the current (for a fixed resistance).

Charge in Circuits

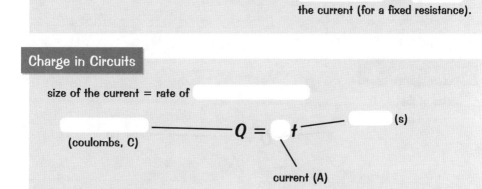

size of the current = rate of [   ]

[   ] (coulombs, C) ——— $Q = \bigcirc t$ ——— [   ] (s)

current (A)

Second Go:
..... / ..... / .....

Current

Current, Potential Difference and Resistance

	Definition	Unit
CURRENT		
POTENTIAL DIFFERENCE		
RESISTANCE		

Current in Circuits

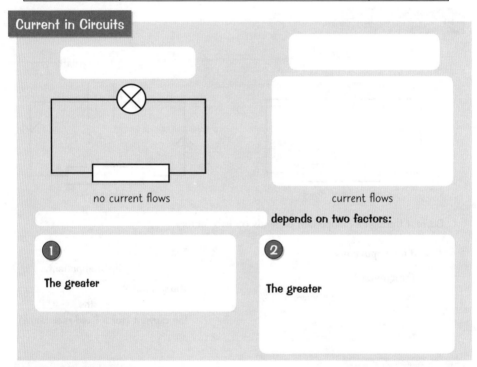

no current flows

current flows

depends on two factors:

1

The greater

2

The greater

Charge in Circuits

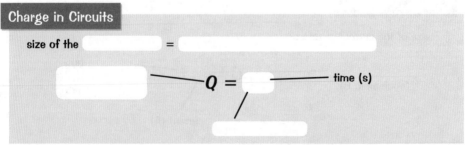

size of the [   ] = [   ]

[   ] — $Q =$ [   ] — time (s)

 ✓ ✓ ✓

V = IR and Circuit Symbols

Potential Difference Equation

potential difference (⬭) ——— $V = IR$ ⟨ ⬭ (Ω)

⬭ (A)

Circuit Symbols

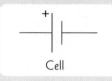

Cell

Battery

....

Voltmeter

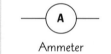
Ammeter

Switch closed

....

Variable resistor

....
....

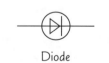
Diode

LDR (Light-
Dependent Resistor)

....

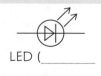
LED (.....................
.....................)

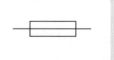
....

Components are connected
by .... —
they represent the wires.

 ✓   ✓   ✓

$V = IR$ and Circuit Symbols

Potential Difference Equation

potential difference (V)

Circuit Symbols

Battery

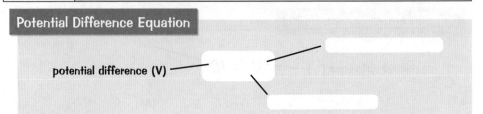

A

LDR (Light-Dependent Resistor)

LED (Light-Emitting Diode)

Components are connected by

 ✓ ✓ ✓

I-V Characteristics & Circuit Devices

Three Different *I-V* Characteristics

1 Ohmic conductor (e.g. a resistor) at constant temperature

Current is [_____]

to potential difference...

... so resistance [_____] .

This graph is ....

Components with changing resistance (when current through them varies):

[_____]   [_____]

2 Filament lamp [_____]

Current increases...

... so [_____]
of filament
increases...

... so resistance
[_____] .

3 Diode [_____]

[_____]
in one direction...

... so current
[_____]
[_____]
[_____] .

These graphs are ....

LDRs and Thermistors

	LDR [__]	Thermistor [__]
depends on...	light intensity	temperature
Lower resistance in...		
Used in...	automatic night lights	

I-V Characteristics & Circuit Devices

Three Different *I-V* Characteristics

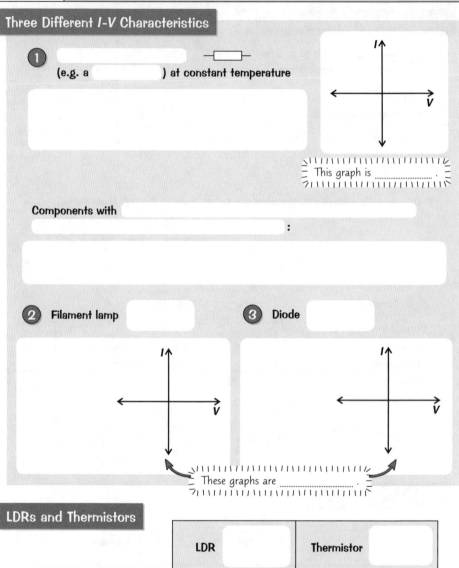

1 ⬚⬚⬚⬚⬚⬚⬚ ▭

(e.g. a ⬚⬚⬚⬚) at constant temperature

This graph is ....

Components with ⬚⬚⬚⬚⬚⬚⬚

⬚⬚⬚⬚⬚⬚⬚ :

2 Filament lamp ⬚⬚⬚

3 Diode ⬚⬚⬚

These graphs are ....

LDRs and Thermistors

	LDR	Thermistor
⬚⬚⬚ depends on...		
Lower resistance in...		
Used in...		

Series and Parallel Circuits

Series Circuits

Current is [_____].

$$I_1 = \boxed{}$$

Total source potential difference is

[_____].

$$V_{total} = \boxed{}$$

Total resistance of components

= [_____].

$$R_{total} = \boxed{}$$

Adding a resistor in series [_____] the total resistance of the circuit.

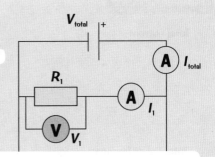

Parallel Circuits

Total current flowing around a
circuit = [_____]

[_____].

$$I_{total} = \boxed{}$$

Potential difference across each
branch is the same as [_____]

[_____].

$$V_1 = V_2 = \boxed{}$$

The total resistance of resistors
in parallel is [_____] the
resistance of the smallest resistor.

Adding a resistor in parallel [_____] the total resistance of the circuit.

34

Series and Parallel Circuits

Series Circuits

Current

[ ] = [ ]

Total source

[ ] = [ ]

Total resistance

[ ] = [ ]

Adding a resistor in series

Parallel Circuits

Total current

[ ] = [ ]

Potential difference

[ ] = [ ] = [ ]

The total resistance of resistors in parallel

Adding a resistor in parallel

Mixed Practice Quizzes

Here are some quick-fire quiz questions to test what you've done on p.27-34.
No — don't mention it. Mark each test yourself and tot up your score.

Quiz 1   Date: ...... / ...... / ......

1) True or false? The *I-V* graph of a diode is linear.
2) What does the circuit symbol '—⊗—' represent?
3) What happens to the total resistance of a circuit
   when another resistor is added to the circuit in series?
4) What is the circuit symbol for a diode?
5) What electrical property is the same on every branch of a parallel circuit?
6) What electrical property is measured in amperes?
7) What happens to the resistance of an LDR when light intensity increases?
8) What shape does the *I-V* graph of an ohmic conductor have?
9) What is the equation for charge flow?
10) What is the circuit symbol for an LDR?

Total:

Quiz 2   Date: ...... / ...... / ......

1) True or false? The total resistance of two resistors in parallel
   is less than the resistance of the smaller of the two resistors.
2) True or false? Potential difference is measured in volts.
3) Give an example of an ohmic conductor.
4) What shape does the *I-V* graph for a diode have?
5) What is the equation that links potential difference, current and resistance?
6) What does the circuit symbol '—Ⓥ—' represent?
7) What does the resistance of a thermistor depend on?
8) How do you calculate the total resistance
   of two resistors connected in series?
9) What must be included in a circuit in order for current to flow?
10) What is the circuit symbol for a cell?

Total:

Mixed Practice Quizzes

Quiz 3   Date: ...... / ...... / ......

1) What does the circuit symbol '—o——o—' represent?
2) Give one application for a thermistor.
3) What electrical property is the same everywhere in a series circuit?
4) What property is measured in coulombs?
5) What are the units of resistance?
6) What will happen to the current through a component if its resistance increases while the potential difference across it stays the same?
7) True or false? An ohmic conductor at a constant temperature has a constant resistance.
8) True or false? Adding another resistor in parallel increases the total resistance of the circuit.
9) Name two circuit devices whose resistance changes when the current through them changes.
10) What is the circuit symbol for a fuse?

Total:

Quiz 4   Date: ...... / ...... / ......

1) What is the circuit symbol for a thermistor?
2) What is electric current?
3) In what type of circuit is the current the same at every point in the circuit?
4) What electrical device has an *I-V* graph that is a straight line through the origin?
5) Name the device whose resistance decreases as the light on it gets brighter.
6) True or false? The size of a current is equal to the rate of flow of charge.
7) State the two factors that the current through a component depends on.
8) What does the circuit symbol '—⊕—' represent?
9) How does adding a resistor in parallel affect the total resistance of a circuit?
10) True or false? The *I-V* graph of a filament lamp is a straight line through the origin.

Total:

Electricity in the Home

Two Types of Electricity Supply

1. [_____] — current that constantly changes direction and is produced by [_____]. Used in mains supply.

2. [_____] — current that always flows in the same direction and is produced by [_____]. Supplied by batteries.

Three Facts about UK Mains

1. [____] supply

2. frequency of [____]

3. voltage around [____]

Three-core Cables

- Most [_____] have a three-core cable.
- The insulation on each wire has a particular [____] to identify it.

[____] (green and yellow)

[____] (blue)

[____] (brown)

	live wire	neutral wire	earth wire
Colour			
Potential difference (V)		around 0	
Use			Stops appliance casing becoming live.

Current only flows through [____] when there's a fault.

Electric Shocks

[____] produced across body.

[____] through body.

Electric shocks can [_____].

Even if a plug socket [_____], there is still danger of an electric shock.

Any connection between [_____] and the [_____] earth can be dangerous — e.g. it could cause a fire.

Topic 2 — Electricity

Electricity in the Home

Two Types of Electricity Supply

① **ALTERNATING CURRENT (   ) —**

② **DIRECT CURRENT (   ) —**

Three Facts about UK Mains

①

②

③

Three-core Cables

-
-

(green and yellow)

(blue)

(brown)

Colour			
Potential difference (V)			
Use			

.... only flows
through ....
when there's a ....

Electric Shocks

Current flows
through
body.

Electric shocks can

Even if a plug socket

Energy, Power and the National Grid

First Go:
..... / ..... / .....

Energy Transfers

When charge flows, (_____)
(and so energy is transferred).

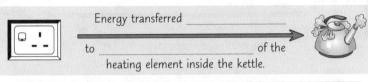

Energy transferred _____
to _____ of the
heating element inside the kettle.

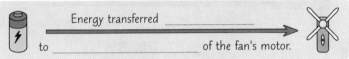

Energy transferred _____
to _____ of the fan's motor.

Energy

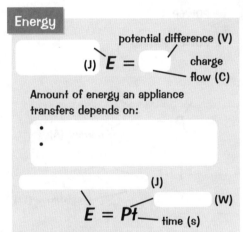

potential difference (V)

(J) $E =$ [ ] charge
flow (C)

Amount of energy an appliance
transfers depends on:

•
•

[ ] (J)

$E = Pt$ — time (s)

[ ] (W)

Power

POWER — [ ] .

POWER RATING — maximum safe power
[ ] .

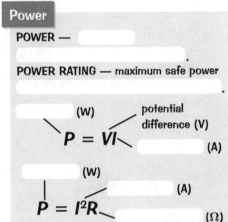

[ ] (W)   potential
difference (V)
$P = VI$
[ ] (A)

[ ] (W)
[ ] (A)
$P = I^2R$
[ ] (Ω)

The National Grid

NATIONAL GRID — a system of ( ) and ( )
that connect power stations to consumers.

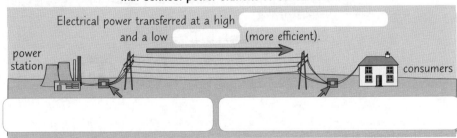

Electrical power transferred at a high [ ]
and a low [ ] (more efficient).

power
station

consumers

[ ]   [ ]

Transferring at a high [ ] would heat up the wires and transfer a lot of
energy to the [ ] of the surroundings (not efficient).

 ✓ ✓ ✓

Second Go:
..... /..... /.....

Energy, Power and the National Grid

Energy Transfers

When charge flows, ⬭ is done (and so energy is transferred).

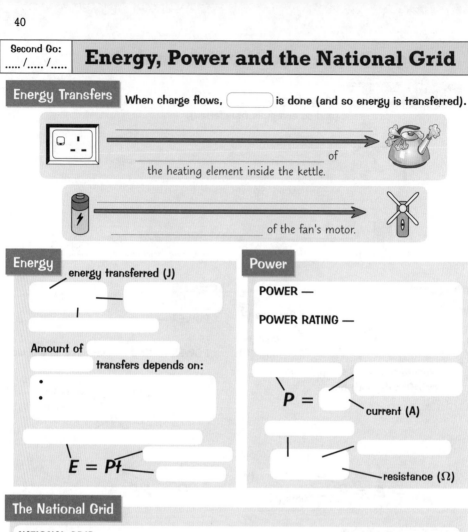

_____ of
the heating element inside the kettle.

_____ of the fan's motor.

Energy

energy transferred (J)

Amount of ⬭ transfers depends on:

•
•

$E = Pt$

Power

POWER —

POWER RATING —

$P =$ ⬭

current (A)

resistance (Ω)

The National Grid

NATIONAL GRID —

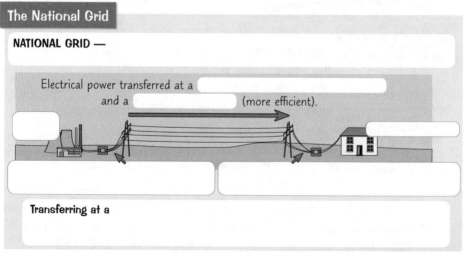

Electrical power transferred at a ⬭
and a ⬭ (more efficient).

Transferring at a

Static Electricity

Static Charges

Rub two _____ _____ together.

_____ move from one to the other.

Both materials become _____ . Charge on each material is _____ .

Only _____ move, _____ don't move.

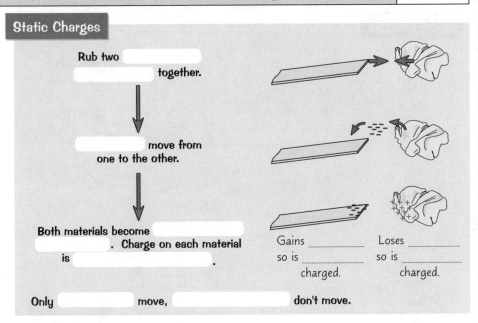

Gains _____ so is _____ charged.

Loses _____ so is _____ charged.

Electric Sparks

ELECTRIC SPARK — the passage of _____ across a gap between a _____ and the _____ (or an _____). (This usually happens when the gap is _____ .)

Three steps to an electric spark:

1 _____ builds on an object.

2 _____ between object and earth (at _____) increases.

3 When _____ is large enough, there is a spark.

Static Electricity

Static Charges

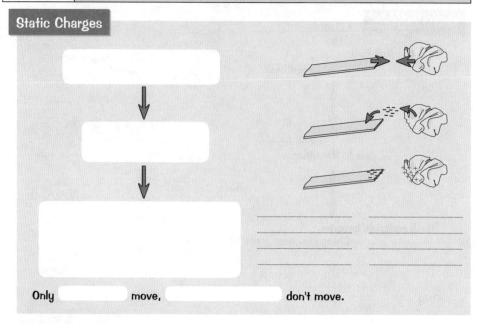

Only _____ move, _____ don't move.

Electric Sparks

ELECTRIC SPARK —

Three steps to an electric spark:

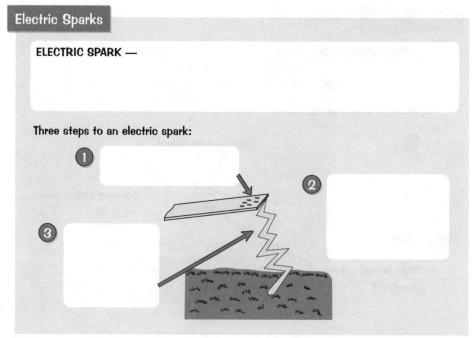

1

2

3

Electric Fields

Electric Fields Around Charged Spheres

ELECTRIC FIELD — a region in which [   ] [   ] feels a [   ]. An electric field is created around any [   ] object.

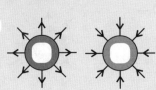

Strong electric fields .... air particles, which can cause ....

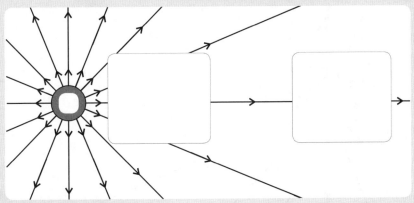

Attraction and Repulsion

When a charged object is placed in the electric field of another charged object, they [   ].

These are ....

[   ] :

[   ] :

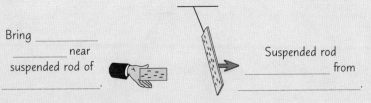

Bring .... near suspended rod of ....

Suspended rod .... from ....

As distance between charged objects decreases, force acting on the charges [   ].

Topic 2 — Electricity

Electric Fields

Electric Fields Around Charged Spheres

ELECTRIC FIELD —

An electric field is created around

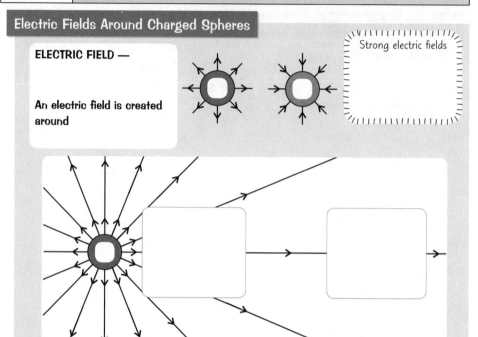

Strong electric fields

Attraction and Repulsion

When a charged object

These are ....
....

Attraction:

Repulsion:

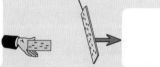

As distance between charged objects

Mixed Practice Quizzes

I hope you're not too frazzled from pages 37-44, because it's time for you to field some quiz questions. Give them a go, mark your test, and see how you did.

Quiz 1   Date: ...... / ...... / ......

1) True or false? Movement of positive charges can cause a build-up of static charge.
2) State the purpose of a step-up transformer in the national grid.
3) What is the equation that links energy transferred, charge flow and potential difference?
4) What is an electric spark?
5) What is meant by the power rating of a device?
6) True or false? It is safe to touch an exposed wire if its plug is turned off.
7) What is meant by alternating current?
8) What is the voltage of the UK mains supply?
9) What is the purpose of the earth wire in an appliance?
10) Describe the forces that act between two positively charged objects.

Total:

Quiz 2   Date: ...... / ...... / ......

1) True or false? Strong electric fields can ionise air, causing a spark.
2) What is the national grid?
3) True or false? The UK mains supply provides direct current.
4) What is the potential difference of the live wire in a UK plug?
5) Describe one energy transfer that occurs when an electric kettle is used.
6) How does distance from a charged object affect the strength of its electric field?
7) Why are the wires of a three-core cable colour coded?
8) State two factors that determine the amount of energy transferred by an appliance.
9) State the equation that links power, current and resistance.
10) What type of static charge is formed when an object gains electrons?

Total:

Topic 2 — Electricity

Mixed Practice Quizzes

Quiz 3 — Date: ...... / ...... / ......

1) Do electric field lines point towards or away from a negatively charged sphere?

2) What device is used to decrease the potential difference of the electricity supply in the national grid?

3) During an electric shock, what happens after a large potential difference is formed across the body?

4) What type of voltage produces direct current?

5) What is the potential difference of the earth wire in a UK plug?

6) How is a positive static charge formed?

7) What is the name for the passage of electrons across a gap between a charged object and the earth?

8) What value is equal to energy transferred per second?

9) True or false? Two objects with opposite electric charges will repel each other.

10) True or false? The earth wire only carries current if there is a fault.

Total:

Quiz 4 — Date: ...... / ...... / ......

1) Why is electrical power transmitted at a low current in the national grid?

2) How are static charges formed when insulating materials rub together?

3) What is the frequency of the UK mains supply?

4) State the equation that links power, potential difference and current.

5) What colour is the neutral wire in a three-core cable?

6) What type of current is constantly changing direction?

7) What is an electric field?

8) True or false? The stronger an electric field, the further apart its field lines.

9) How would a suspended negatively charged rod move if a negatively charged object was brought close to it?

10) What is the purpose of the live wire in a three-core cable?

Total:

Density, States and Internal Energy

Density

DENSITY — [   ]

[   ]

$\rho = \dfrac{m}{V}$ — mass (kg)

— volume ([ ])

States of Matter

Density ↓

	Particle arrangement	Forces between particles	Distance between particles	Particle motion
SOLID		Strong		Vibration only
LIQUID	Irregular	Weak		
GAS			Large	

Changes of State

Changes of state are [   ]. [   ] is always conserved.

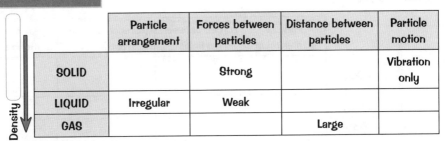

melt

sublimate

gas

or
evaporate

Internal Energy

INTERNAL ENERGY — the total energy stored by the [   ] that make up a [   ].

Internal energy of a system
= total [   ]
in [   ]
energy stores of all its particles

Heating

Heating increases the [   ] of a system.

This can do one of two things:

1 Increase the [   ]

2 Change the [   ]

Second Go:
...... / ...... / ......

Density, States and Internal Energy

Density

DENSITY —

density (kg/m³)

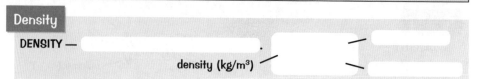

States of Matter

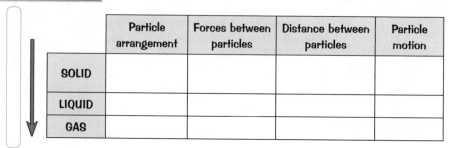

	Particle arrangement	Forces between particles	Distance between particles	Particle motion
SOLID				
LIQUID				
GAS				

Changes of State

Changes of state ....

....

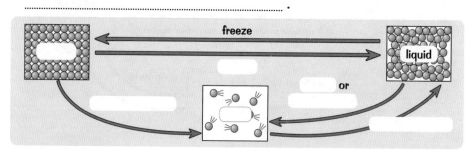

freeze

liquid

or

Internal Energy

INTERNAL ENERGY —

Internal energy of a system =

Heating

Heating increases

This can do one of two things:

 1

 2

Heating and Cooling

Heating Graphs

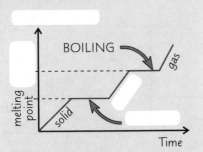

Three things happen in melting and boiling:

1. _____ between particles are broken.

2. Internal energy increases — energy is transferred _____ .

3. Temperature _____

Cooling Graphs

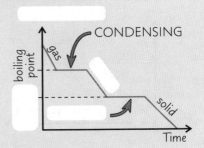

Three things happen in condensing and freezing:

1. Stronger _____ between particles.

2. Internal energy decreases — energy is transferred _____

3. Temperature _____

Specific Heat Capacity, Latent Heat and Specific Latent Heat

SPECIFIC HEAT CAPACITY — the amount of energy needed to raise _____ .

LATENT HEAT — the energy needed to _____ .

SPECIFIC LATENT HEAT — the amount of energy needed to change _____ ,

without changing _____ .

SPECIFIC LATENT HEAT OF _____ — the specific latent heat of changing between a solid _____ .

SPECIFIC LATENT HEAT OF VAPORISATION — the specific latent heat of changing _____ .

Topic 3 — Particle Model of Matter

Heating and Cooling

Heating Graphs

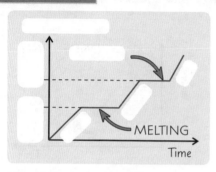

MELTING

Time

Three things happen in melting
and boiling:

 1

 2

 3

Cooling Graphs

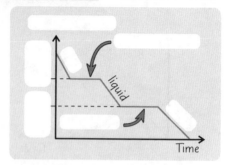

liquid

Time

Three things happen in condensing
and freezing:

 1

 2

3

Specific Heat Capacity, Latent Heat and Specific Latent Heat

SPECIFIC HEAT CAPACITY —

LATENT HEAT —

SPECIFIC LATENT HEAT —

SPECIFIC LATENT HEAT OF FUSION —

SPECIFIC LATENT HEAT OF VAPORISATION —

Particle Motion in Gases

Gas Particles and Gas Pressure

The higher the [_____] of a gas, the higher
the [_____] in the kinetic energy
stores of the gas particles.

Gas particles are
....
....
....

Gas pressure is caused by [____]

with a surface and exerting a

[_____] .

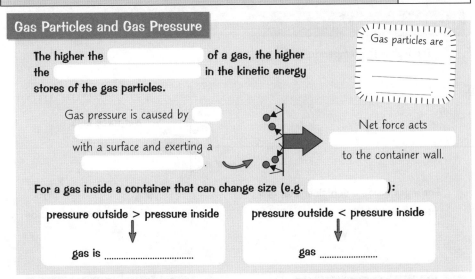

Net force acts

[_____]

to the container wall.

For a gas inside a container that can change size (e.g. [_____]):

pressure outside > pressure inside

⬇

gas is ....

pressure outside < pressure inside

⬇

gas ....

A Gas at Constant Volume

Temperature increase

⬇

Particles get [_____]

[_____]

[_____]

more often.

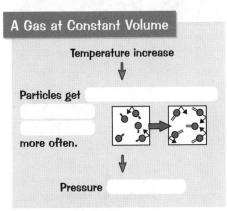

⬇

Pressure [_____]

A Gas at Constant Temperature

Volume increase

⬇

Particles [_____]

[_____]

[_____]

less often.

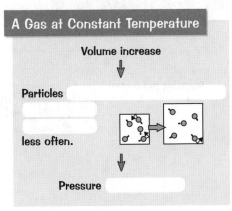

⬇

Pressure [_____]

Doing Work on Gases

[_____] is applied to gas.

[_____] as
energy is transferred.

➡

[_____] on
the gas increases its
[_____] .

➡

[_____] of an enclosed gas

[_____] .

.... is applied to
air in ....
....

➡

....
of air in tyre increases.

➡

Tyre temperature
....

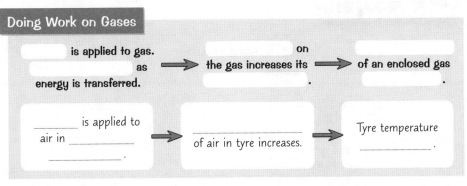

Particle Motion in Gases

Gas Particles and Gas Pressure

The higher the temperature of a gas,

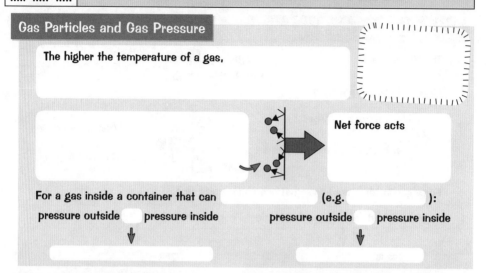

Net force acts

For a gas inside a container that can _____ (e.g. _____):

pressure outside ⬚ pressure inside   pressure outside ⬚ pressure inside

A Gas at Constant Volume

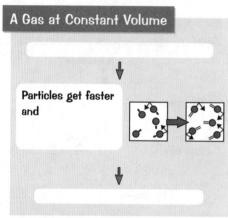

Particles get faster and

A Gas at Constant Temperature

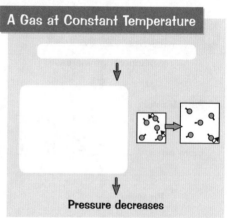

Pressure decreases

Doing Work on Gases

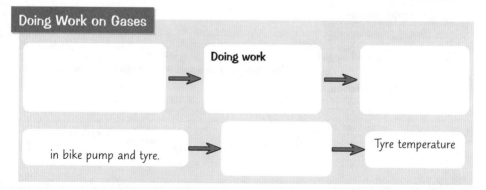

Doing work

in bike pump and tyre.

Tyre temperature

Mixed Practice Quizzes

Keep your cool — have a go at these quiz questions which test you on pages 47-52. Tick off the questions you get right to work out your total.

Quiz 1   Date: ...... / ...... / ......

1) True or false? The internal energy of a system is equal to the total energy in the kinetic energy stores of the particles. ☑

2) Does an upwards slope on a heating graph show a temperature change or a change in state? ☑

3) State what happens to the temperature of a substance as it condenses. ☑

4) Which usually has a lower density — a solid or a liquid? ☑

5) What is meant by latent heat? ☑

6) Give the formula for density. ☑

7) True or false? Mass is always conserved during changes of state. ☑

8) Which state of matter has the biggest distance between its particles? ☑

9) Give the definition of specific heat capacity. ☑

10) In which direction does the net force of gas particles act on a surface? ☑

Total:

Quiz 2   Date: ...... / ...... / ......

1) Explain what happens to the pressure of a gas if you increase its temperature whilst keeping it at a constant volume. ☑

2) Between which two states of matter does freezing occur? ☑

3) Give the definition of specific latent heat. ☑

4) True or false? Gas particles are constantly randomly moving. ☑

5) True or false? Changes of state are chemical changes. ☑

6) What happens to the internal energy of a gas if work is done on it? ☑

7) Which has a higher density — a liquid or a gas? ☑

8) Describe the particle motion of particles in a solid. ☑

9) What happens to the air in an air-filled balloon if the air pressure is greater on the inside of the balloon than on the outside? ☑

10) True or false? The flat parts of a heating graph show a change of state. ☑

Total:

Mixed Practice Quizzes

Date: ...... / ...... / ......

1) What is the difference between specific
   heat capacity and specific latent heat?

2) True or false? Heating a substance always increases its temperature.

3) Name the term given for a gas turning into a liquid.

4) Give the definition for the specific latent heat of fusion.

5) If work is done on an enclosed gas, what can happen to its temperature?

6) State what happens to the internal energy of a substance as it boils.

7) What is meant by the density of a substance?

8) What is meant by the internal energy of a system?

9) Does a downwards slope on a cooling graph show
   a temperature change or a change in state?

10) Describe the motion of gas particles.

Total:

Quiz 4   Date: ...... / ...... / ......

1) Can increasing the internal energy of a system cause a change of state?

2) Describe the particle arrangement of particles in solids, liquids and gases.

3) Explain why pumping a tyre with air can cause the tyre to heat up.

4) True or false? Bonds between particles
   are broken when a substance is melting.

5) What is meant by sublimation?

6) Give the definition for the specific latent heat of vaporisation.

7) Explain what happens to the pressure of a gas if you increase
   its volume whilst keeping it at a constant temperature.

8) What is it called when a solid turns into a liquid?

9) True or false? The melting point of a substance is the temperature
   at which a gas of the substance can turn into a liquid.

10) What happens to the average energy in the kinetic energy stores
    of gas particles if the temperature of the gas is increased?

Total:

Topic 3 — Particle Model of Matter

Developing the Model of the Atom

First Go:
..... /..... /.....

The History of the Atom

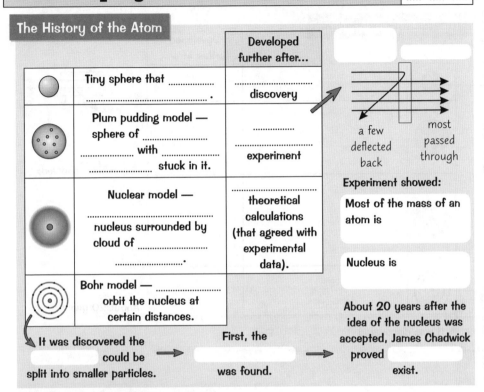

		Developed further after...	
⬤	Tiny sphere that	.... discovery	
(plum pudding)	Plum pudding model — sphere of .... with .... stuck in it.	.... experiment	
(nuclear)	Nuclear model — .... nucleus surrounded by cloud of	theoretical calculations (that agreed with experimental data).	
(Bohr)	Bohr model — .... orbit the nucleus at certain distances.		

a few deflected back   most passed through

Experiment showed:

Most of the mass of an atom is

Nucleus is

It was discovered the [   ] could be split into smaller particles.   ➡   First, the [   ] was found.   ➡   About 20 years after the idea of the nucleus was accepted, James Chadwick proved [   ] exist.

The Current Model of the Atom

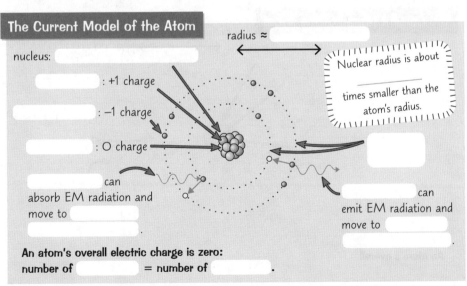

radius ≈ [   ]

nucleus: [   ]

[   ] : +1 charge

[   ] : −1 charge

[   ] : 0 charge

[   ] can absorb EM radiation and move to [   ]

Nuclear radius is about .... times smaller than the atom's radius.

[   ] can emit EM radiation and move to [   ]

An atom's overall electric charge is zero:
number of [   ] = number of [   ] .

Developing the Model of the Atom

The History of the Atom

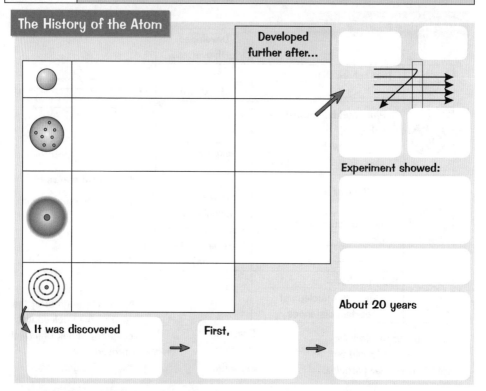

		Developed further after...

Experiment showed:

About 20 years

It was discovered

First,

The Current Model of the Atom

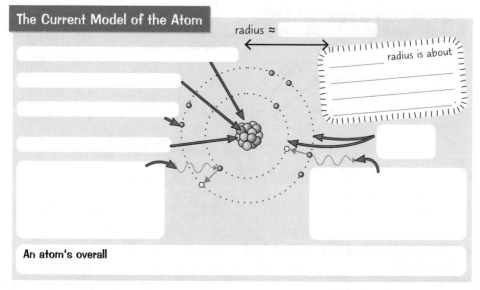

radius ≈

radius is about

An atom's overall

Isotopes and Nuclear Radiation

Mass Number and Atomic Number

All atoms of each element have ....

ISOTOPES of an element — atoms with the same number of .... but different numbers of ....

.... — total number of .... and .... in an atom.

$^{16}_{8}O$

.... — number of .... in an atom (equal to .... of nucleus).

Types of Nuclear Radiation

RADIOACTIVE DECAY — when an unstable nucleus .... into .... and gives out .... to become more stable.

Unstable nuclei can also release .... when they decay.

IONISING RADIATION (α, β and γ) — radiation that knocks .... off atoms, creating ....

	.... (α)	.... (β)	.... (γ)
Consists of...	2 .... and 2 .... (................ nucleus)	fast-moving .... from nucleus	.... from nucleus
Absorbed by...	Sheet of	Sheet of	Thick sheets of ....
Range in air	Few	Few	
Ionising power		Moderate	
Example of use			Medical tracers

Nuclear Equations

γ-decay   mass and charge ....

α-decay
• mass ....
• charge ....

$^{238}_{92}U \longrightarrow \boxed{} Th + {}^{4}_{2}He$

β-decay
• mass ....
• charge ....

$^{14}_{6}C \longrightarrow \boxed{} N + {}^{0}_{-1}e$

During ...., a neutron in the nucleus turns into a ....

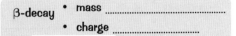

Second Go:
..... /..... /.....

Isotopes and Nuclear Radiation

Mass Number and Atomic Number

ISOTOPES of an element —

All atoms of each element ....

$$^{16}_{\ 8}O$$

Types of Nuclear Radiation

RADIOACTIVE DECAY —

Unstable nuclei can also

IONISING RADIATION (α, β and γ) —

	(α)	(β)	(γ)
Consists of...			
Absorbed by...			
Range in air			
Ionising power			
Example of use			

Nuclear Equations

γ-decay ....

α-decay • ....
• ....

$$^{238}_{\ 92}U \longrightarrow \quad Th + \qquad /$$

β-decay • ....
• ....

$$^{14}_{\ 6}C \longrightarrow \quad N + \qquad /$$

During ...., a neutron ....

  ☑ ☑ ☑

Radioactivity and Risk

Activity and Count-Rate

ACTIVITY — the [____] at which a source [____], measured in becquerels (Bq).

COUNT-RATE — the [____] reaching a detector [____].

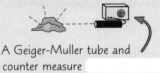

A Geiger-Muller tube and counter measure [____].

Contamination and Irradiation

RADIOACTIVE CONTAMINATION — getting unwanted radioactive atoms [____].

IRRADIATION — the [____] to nuclear radiation ([____]).

Three precautions to protect against [____]:

1 Keep sources in [____]

2 [____] barriers or be in [____] to the source.

3 [____] with remote-controlled arms.

Half-life

Radioactive decay is [____].

HALF-LIFE — time taken for [____] to halve.

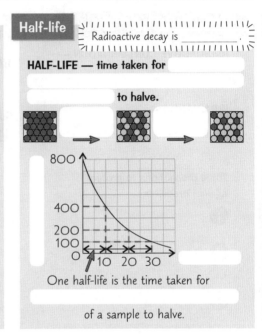

800
400
200
100
0   10 20 30

One half-life is the time taken for [____] of a sample to halve.

Risk of Radiation

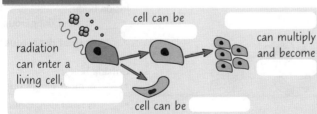

radiation can enter a living cell, [____]

cell can be [____]

can multiply and become [____]

cell can be [____]

Inside body:
• ...... is most dangerous
• ...... is least dangerous

Outside body:
• ...... is most dangerous
• ...... is least dangerous

• An isotope with a short half-life [____] — emits [____] of radiation to start with but quickly [____].

• An isotope with a long half-life [____] — emits [____] of radiation for [____] so nearby areas are exposed for a long time.

Radioactivity and Risk

Activity and Count-Rate

ACTIVITY —

COUNT-RATE —

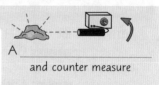

A _____

and counter measure

_____ .

Contamination and Irradiation

RADIOACTIVE CONTAMINATION —

IRRADIATION —

Three precautions to protect against irradiation:

1

2

3

Half-life

Radioactive decay is _____ .

HALF-LIFE —

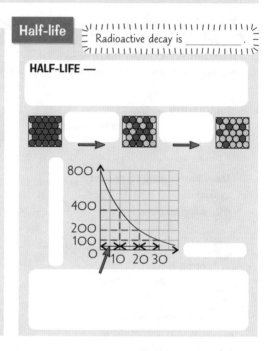

Risk of Radiation

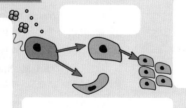

Inside body:
- .... is most dangerous
- .... is least dangerous

Outside body:
- .... is most dangerous
- .... is least dangerous

- **An isotope with a short half-life**

- **An isotope with a long half-life**

Background Radiation and Uses

Background Radiation

BACKGROUND RADIATION — [_____]
radiation that's [_____].

Two types of sources:

1 Natural sources — [_____]

2 Man-made sources — [_____]

Radiation Dose

RADIATION DOSE — measure of
[_____]
[_____] **due to** [_____]
[_____].

Depends on:

• [_____]

• [_____]

Medical Uses

Two ways ionising radiation is used in
radiotherapy to [_____]:

1 [_____] from outside
body directed at [_____].

2 [_____] used in medical
implants put inside body next to
[_____].

[_____] (radioactive
source) injected into patient to explore
[_____]

[_____] detected outside
the body.

[_____] used
so that radiation passes out of body.

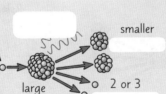

Nuclear Fission

NUCLEAR FISSION — splitting a [_____] (e.g. uranium
or plutonium) into [_____] of approximately the same size.

Fission usually occurs
after an unstable
[_____] absorbs
[_____].
(Spontaneous fission
rarely happens.)

large

smaller

2 or 3

Released [_____] can be
absorbed by another nucleus,
starting a [_____] ...

... [_____] in
nuclear reactor.

... [_____]
in nuclear explosion.

Energy released as [_____] and in [_____] energy stores of fission products.

Nuclear Fusion

NUCLEAR FUSION — two light
[_____] collide at high speed
and join [_____].

lighter

Some of the [_____]
[_____] is converted
into energy, which can be
released as [_____]

Background Radiation and Uses

Background Radiation

BACKGROUND RADIATION —

Two types of sources:

1

2

Radiation Dose

RADIATION DOSE —

Depends on:

•

•

Medical Uses

Two ways _____ is used in
radiotherapy to _____ :

1

2

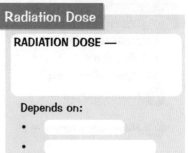

Nuclear Fission

NUCLEAR FISSION —

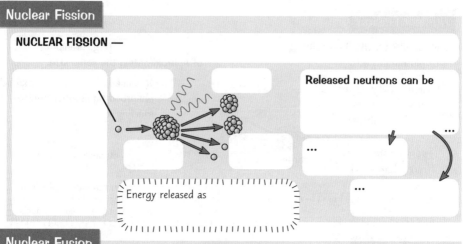

Released neutrons can be

...

...

...

Energy released as

Nuclear Fusion

NUCLEAR FUSION —

lighter

Some of the

Mixed Practice Quizzes

Before all that revision from p.55-62 decays out of your brain, have a go at these quizzes. When you finish each quiz, check your answers and work out your score.

Quiz 1

Date: ...... / ...... / ......

1) True or false? The mass of a nucleus decreases when it emits an alpha particle.
2) What is meant by the activity of a radioactive source?
3) Which model of the atom was adopted after the plum pudding model?
4) True or false? The nucleus of an atom is negatively charged.
5) Which type of ionising radiation has the longest range in air?
6) What is the approximate radius of an atom?
7) What is beta radiation made up of?
8) What name is given to the number of protons in an atom?
9) Which type of ionising radiation is most dangerous inside the body?
10) Describe how medical tracers are used.

Total:

Quiz 2

Date: ...... / ...... / ......

1) What does an electron need to absorb to move to a higher energy level in an atom?
2) What are isotopes of an element?
3) True or false? Mass may be converted into energy during nuclear fusion.
4) What evidence caused the nuclear model of the atom to develop into the Bohr model of the atom?
5) Which type of nuclear radiation is made up of a helium nucleus?
6) What is meant by irradiation?
7) True or false? Half-life is equal to the time taken for the activity of a sample to fall to half of its initial level.
8) State the products of nuclear fission.
9) What happens to the charge on a nucleus when it emits a beta particle?
10) Give two examples of natural sources of background radiation.

Total:

Topic 4 — Atomic Structure

Mixed Practice Quizzes

Quiz 3 — Date: ...... / ...... / ......

1) True or false? When a nucleus emits gamma radiation, its charge decreases.
2) What does a Geiger-Muller tube and counter measure?
3) What is the charge on an electron?
4) What did the alpha particle scattering experiment prove about the atom?
5) What is meant by radiation dose?
6) How many times smaller is the radius of a nucleus compared to the radius of an atom?
7) What does the mass number of an atom tell you?
8) Give one precaution you could take to protect against irradiation.
9) What particle can trigger nuclear fission when it is absorbed by a large nucleus?
10) Which type of nuclear radiation has the highest ionising power?

Total:

Quiz 4 — Date: ...... / ...... / ......

1) True or false? All atoms of the same element have the same number of neutrons.
2) True or false? An isotope with a short half-life will decay quickly.
3) What two particles make up the nucleus of an atom?
4) What is meant by radioactive decay?
5) Which type of nuclear radiation is absorbed by a sheet of paper?
6) Give two factors that affect the radiation dose a person receives.
7) During which type of radioactive decay does a neutron in the nucleus turn into a proton?
8) What causes a nuclear chain reaction?
9) What is meant by radioactive contamination?
10) Describe the plum pudding model of the atom.

Total:

Topic 4 — Atomic Structure

Scalars, Vectors, Forces and Weight

First Go: ...../...../.....

Scalars

SCALAR QUANTITIES —

- [____]
- mass
- distance
- [____]
- [____]

Vectors

VECTOR QUANTITIES —

- force
- [____]
- momentum
- [____]
- acceleration

Direction of arrow shows _____.

Length of arrow shows _____.

Forces

FORCE — a push or a pull on an object caused by [____].

Two types of forces:

1 [____] : objects have to be touching.

- [____]
- tension
- [____]
- normal contact force

2 [____] : objects don't need to be touching.

- gravitational force
- [____]
- [____]

Weight, Mass and Gravity

WEIGHT — force that acts on an object due to [____].

Near Earth, weight is caused by [____].

weight (N)

$$W = mg$$

[____]

Weight and mass are [____]

Measure weight with [____]

CENTRE OF MASS — point at which an object's [____] to act.

- Object weight depends on [____] of gravitational field at object location.
- [____] has same value anywhere in the universe.

Second Go:
..... / ..... / .....

Scalars, Vectors, Forces and Weight

Scalars

SCALAR QUANTITIES —

-
-
-
-
- **time**

Vectors

VECTOR QUANTITIES —

-
-
-
-

Direction of

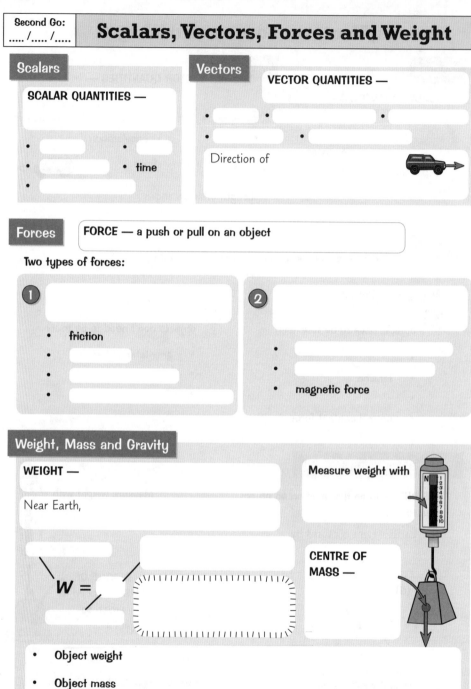

Forces

FORCE — a push or pull on an object

Two types of forces:

1

- friction
-
-
-

2

-
-
- magnetic force

Weight, Mass and Gravity

WEIGHT —

Near Earth,

$W =$ [ ]

Measure weight with

CENTRE OF MASS —

- Object weight
- Object mass

 ✓ ✓ ✓

Calculating Forces and Work Done

Free Body Diagrams

FREE BODY DIAGRAM — shows all forces acting on [_____] .

drag

weight

Arrows show relative [_____] and [_____] of forces acting.

Resolving Forces

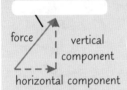

force

vertical component

horizontal component

[_____] forces acting together have [_____] as the single force.

Equilibrium

EQUILIBRIUM — when the forces acting on an object are [_____] and the resultant force [_____] .

Object in [_____]

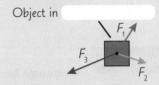

Drawing forces [_____] in scale drawing creates a [_____] .

Two Ways to Calculate Resultant Force

RESULTANT FORCE — a .... force that can .... on an object to give the .... as all the original forces acting together.

1 Add forces pointing in [_____] . Subtract forces pointing in [_____] .

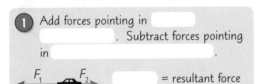

F_1 F_2 [_____] = resultant force

2 Draw forces to [_____] and [_____] .

F_2

F_1

Measure [_____] of resultant force to find its magnitude, and [_____] to find its direction.

Work Done

When a force moves an object from one point to another, energy is [_____] and work is done on the object.

work done (J)
(1 joule =
[_____])

$$W = [\ ]\ s$$

force (N)

distance (moved along [_____])
(m)

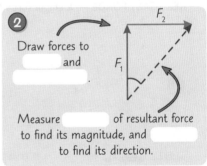

Box does work against [_____]

[_____] causing temperature of box to increase.

Force [_____] on box and energy is transferred to box's [_____] energy store.

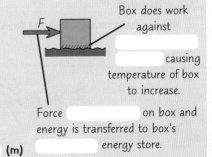

 ✓   ✓   ✓

Topic 5 — Forces

Second Go:
..... / ..... / .....

Calculating Forces and Work Done

Free Body Diagrams

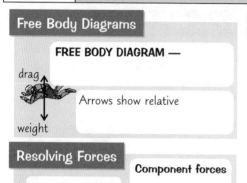

FREE BODY DIAGRAM —

drag

weight

Arrows show relative

Resolving Forces

Component forces

force   vertical
         component

Equilibrium

EQUILIBRIUM —

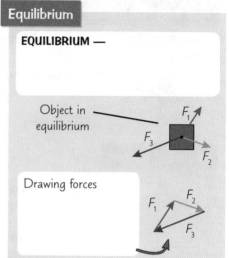

Object in
equilibrium

F_1

F_3

F_2

Drawing forces

F_1 F_2

F_3

Two Ways to Calculate Resultant Force

RESULTANT FORCE — a single force that can

1

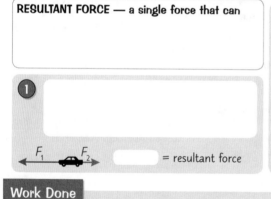

F_1 F_2 = resultant force

2

Draw forces

F_1

Measure

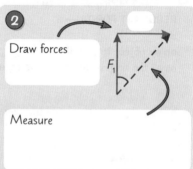

Work Done

When a force moves an object from one point to
another,

$$W = Fs$$

distance (

) (m)

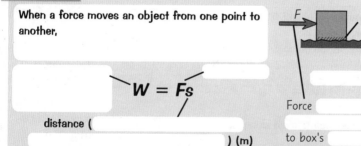

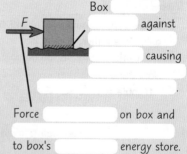

Box

against

causing

.

Force   on box and

to box's   energy store.

 ✓ ✓ ✓

Mixed Practice Quizzes

You've really got some good work done over the last few pages. Time to put your knowledge to the test with some quiz questions covering p.65-68.

Quiz 1   Date: ...... / ...... / ......

1) True or false? Vector quantities have magnitude only.

2) Describe how scale drawings can be used to find the resultant force acting on an object.

3) Give two examples of scalar quantities.

4) Apart from its mass, what does the weight of an object depend on?

5) What is another name for a newtonmeter? What does it measure?

6) Give two examples of contact forces.

7) What does *s* stand for in the formula for calculating work done?

8) What is the name for the force that acts on an object due to gravity?

9) What is a free body diagram?

10) In terms of the forces acting on an object, what does it mean when an object is said to be in equilibrium?

Total:

Quiz 2   Date: ...... / ...... / ......

1) 1 newton metre is equal to how many joules of work?

2) Describe the energy transfers that take place when work is done by a force to move an object from one point to another.

3) What is meant by a resultant force?

4) What does the length of a vector arrow tell you about the vector quantity?

5) What type of force does the gravitational field around Earth cause?

6) What is meant by the centre of mass of an object?

7) Describe the difference between contact and non-contact forces.

8) True or false? Force is a vector quantity.

9) How would you calculate the resultant force acting on an object if all the forces acting on it are on the same line?

10) What are the units for work done?

Total:

Mixed Practice Quizzes

Quiz 3   Date: ...... / ...... / ......

1) What does the direction of a vector arrow tell you about a vector quantity? ☑

2) True or false? When a force moves an object from one point to another, the object does work against frictional forces. ☑

3) True or false? Weight has the units N/kg. ☑

4) Give the equation for calculating the weight of an object, defining each symbol used. ☑

5) Are friction and tension examples of contact forces or non-contact forces? ☑

6) What type of drawing can be used for resolving forces? ☑

7) If all the forces acting on an object in equilibrium are drawn tip-to-tail in a scale drawing, will they create a closed loop or an open loop? ☑

8) Describe the difference between scalar and vector quantities. ☑

9) What is the equation for calculating the work done by a force on an object? ☑

10) What name is given to the force that can replace all the forces acting on an object, to give the same effect as all the original forces acting together? ☑

Total: ☐

Quiz 4   Date: ...... / ...... / ......

1) What is a force? ☑

2) What is gravitational field strength measured in? ☑

3) True or false? Scalar quantities have a magnitude and a direction. ☑

4) Name a piece of apparatus that can be used to measure weight. ☑

5) What type of diagram shows all the forces acting on an isolated object? ☑

6) Give two examples of non-contact forces. ☑

7) True or false? The weight and mass of an object are directly proportional. ☑

8) Give three examples of vector quantities. ☑

9) What is the resultant force acting on an object in equilibrium? ☑

10) Give two ways to calculate the resultant force acting on an object. ☑

Total: ☐

Forces and Elasticity

Changing Shape

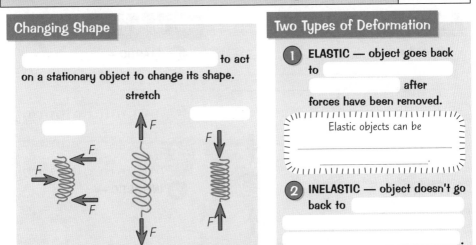

[_____] to act on a stationary object to change its shape.

stretch

F → F
F ← F

F ↓
F ↑

Two Types of Deformation

1. **ELASTIC** — object goes back to [_____] [_____] after forces have been removed.

Elastic objects can be
_____
_____ .

2. **INELASTIC** — object doesn't go back to [_____]

[_____]

[_____] .

Force-Extension Relationship for an Elastic Object

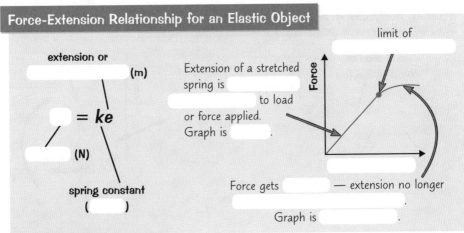

extension or
[_____] (m)

[__] $= ke$

[__] (N)

spring constant
([__])

Extension of a stretched spring is [_____] [_____] to load or force applied.
Graph is [_____].

limit of [_____]

Force

Force gets [_____] — extension no longer [_____]

Graph is [_____].

Work Done and Elasticity

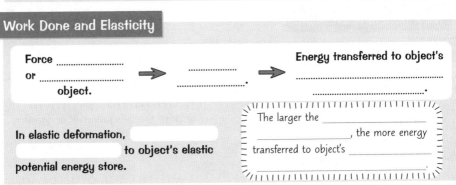

Force ....
or ....
object.

→ .... →

Energy transferred to object's ....
....

In elastic deformation, [_____] [_____] to object's elastic potential energy store.

The larger the ...., the more energy transferred to object's ....

Forces and Elasticity

Changing Shape

More than one ....
....
....

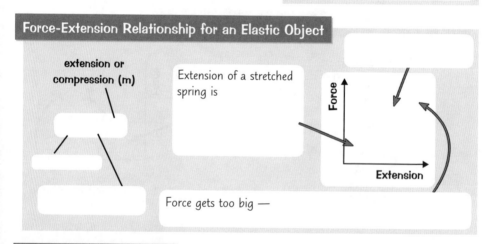

Two Types of Deformation

1 ELASTIC —

2 INELASTIC —

Force-Extension Relationship for an Elastic Object

extension or
compression (m)

Extension of a stretched
spring is

Force gets too big —

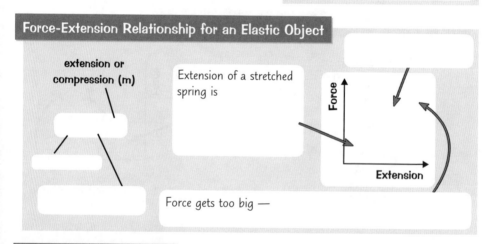

Work Done and Elasticity

Force → → Energy

In elastic deformation, ...
....
....
....

The larger the spring constant or extension,

Moments

Calculating Moments

MOMENT — [ ]

[ ] .

moment of a
force ([ ]) [ ]

$M = Fd$

[ ] distance from the
[ ] to the line of action of the force ([ ])

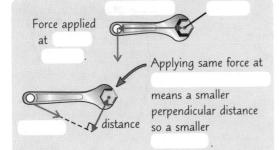

Force applied
at [ ] .

Applying same force at [ ]

means a smaller
perpendicular distance
so a smaller [ ]

[ ] distance .

Balanced Moments

If total [ ]

[ ] equals

[ ] about a [ ] ,
object is balanced.

Smaller mass produces [ ] ...

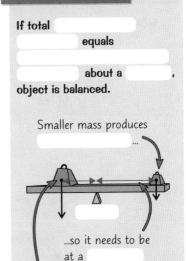

[ ]

...so it needs to be
at a [ ] from pivot...

...to [ ]
bigger mass.

Gears

GEARS — used to transmit the

[ ]

[ ] from
one place to another.

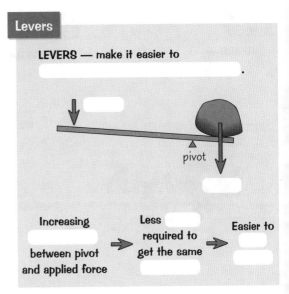

[ ] teeth

Larger gears cause [ ]
moments but turn [ ] .

Levers

LEVERS — make it easier to

[ ] .

[ ]

pivot

[ ]

Increasing
[ ]
between pivot
and applied force

→

Less [ ]
required to
get the same [ ]

→

Easier to
[ ]

 ✓ ✓ ✓

Second Go:
..... / ..... / .....

Moments

Calculating Moments

MOMENT —

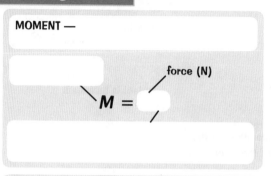

$$M = \boxed{}$$

force (N)

Force

pivot

Applying same force at

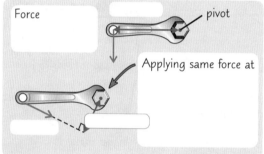

Balanced Moments

If total

Smaller mass produces smaller force...

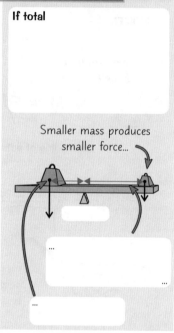

...

...

...

Gears

GEARS —

Levers

LEVERS —

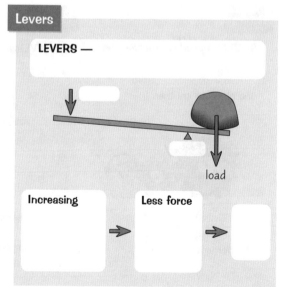

load

Increasing

Less force

Fluid Pressure and Upthrust

Calculating Pressure

Pressure of a fluid means a [____] is exerted [____] to any surface in [____] with the fluid.

pressure
([ ])

A fluid is either [____]

$$p = \frac{F}{A}$$

force [____] to a surface (N)

[____] of that surface ([ ])

Pressure Differences in a Liquid

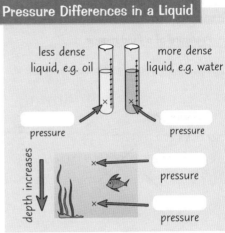

less dense liquid, e.g. oil

more dense liquid, e.g. water

[____] pressure

[____] pressure

depth increases

[____] pressure

[____] pressure

Upthrust

UPTHRUST — the [____] on an object submerged in liquid, due to the [____] of the liquid being greater at the [____] of the object than at the [____].

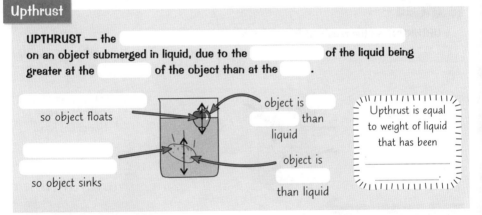

[____]
so object floats

[____]
so object sinks

object is [____] than liquid

object is [____] than liquid

Upthrust is equal to weight of liquid that has been [____]

Atmospheric Pressure

THE ATMOSPHERE — [____] that surrounds the earth.

Atmospheric pressure is created on a surface by [____]

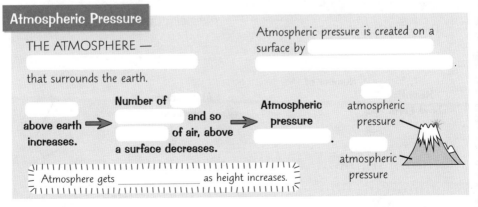

[____]
above earth increases.

Number of [____] and so [____] of air, above a surface decreases.

Atmospheric pressure [____].

[____] atmospheric pressure

[____] atmospheric pressure

Atmosphere gets _____ as height increases.

Fluid Pressure and Upthrust

Calculating Pressure

Pressure of a fluid means

pressure (Pa)

$$p = \underline{}$$

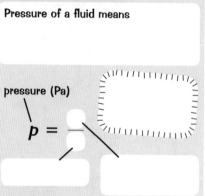

Pressure Differences in a Liquid

liquid, e.g. oil

liquid, e.g. water

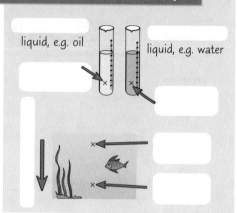

Upthrust

UPTHRUST — the resultant force acting

Upthrust is equal to
weight of liquid

Atmospheric Pressure

THE ATMOSPHERE —

Atmospheric pressure is

Height
above Earth ➡

Number of

Atmospheric
pressure ➡

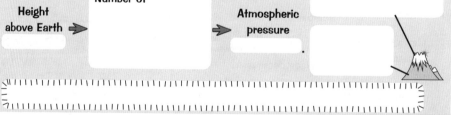

Mixed Practice Quizzes

Doing these quiz questions that cover p.71-76 will really help with exam pressure.

Quiz 1   Date: ...... / ...... / ......

1) What is meant by upthrust?

2) True or false? Only one force has to act on a stationary object to change its shape.

3) Does a graph showing the force-extension relationship of an elastic object become linear or non-linear after the limit of proportionality?

4) Describe how using a lever could make lifting a load easier.

5) True or false? A gas is a fluid.

6) Describe how pressure changes with the depth of a liquid.

7) What is the equation for calculating the moment of a force?

8) What is meant by inelastic deformation?

9) What is the atmosphere?

10) True or false? In elastic deformation, work is done and half of the energy is transferred to the object's elastic potential energy store.

Total:

Quiz 2   Date: ...... / ...... / ......

1) Describe the difference between elastic and inelastic deformation.

2) What is the equation that links force, spring constant and extension?

3) Give the units for the moment of a force.

4) How does a lever reduce the force required to get the same moment?

5) What quantity has the units Pa?

6) At what angle does fluid pressure exert a force on a surface in contact with the fluid?

7) Does the amount of energy stored in the elastic potential energy store of an object increase or decrease with an increase in the object's extension?

8) What does the d stand for in $M = Fd$?

9) Does the atmosphere get more or less dense with an increase in height?

10) Give one factor that affects whether an object floats or sinks in a liquid.

Total:

Mixed Practice Quizzes

Quiz 3   Date: ...... / ...... / ......

1) True or false? Larger gears cause smaller moments.

2) What creates atmospheric pressure?

3) True or false? The extension of a stretched spring is inversely proportional to the force applied to the spring.

4) Which energy store is energy transferred to in elastic deformation?

5) The shape of an object can be changed by bending or stretching the object. Give one other way that the shape of an object can be changed.

6) If an object is balanced, what must be true about the moments acting on it?

7) Describe the shape of a force-extension graph for an elastic object.

8) True or false? Gears are used to transmit the rotational effect of a force from one place to another.

9) If the upthrust acting on an object is equal to its weight, will the object float or sink?

10) Explain why atmospheric pressure decreases as height increases.

Total:

Quiz 4   Date: ...... / ...... / ......

1) State the equation used to calculate pressure at the surface of a fluid.

2) If an object is denser than a liquid, will the object float or sink?

3) What is meant by elastic deformation?

4) What is a spring constant measured in?

5) True or false? The atmosphere gets more dense with an increase in height.

6) Define the moment of a force.

7) If one liquid has a higher density than another liquid, which liquid will have a higher pressure at a certain depth?

8) What are gears used for?

9) Is the atmospheric pressure higher at the top or the bottom of a mountain?

10) If the distance is increased between a pivot and an applied force, is it harder or easier to lift a load?

Total:

Motion

Distance and Displacement

DISTANCE (scalar) —

[_____]

[_____]

(not including its

[_____]).

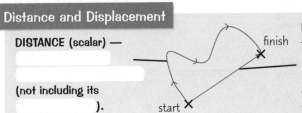

start ✗

finish ✗

DISPLACEMENT (vector) —
the [_____] and the

[_____] from an
object's starting point to its
finishing point.

Speed

SPEED (scalar) — how [_____] you're
going with no regard to [_____].

[_____] — [ ] = vt

(m)

time (s)

speed ([___])

People's walking, running and
cycling speed can be affected by:

- [_____]
- age
- [_____]
- type of ground

Objects, [_____]
rarely travel at a constant speed.

	Typical speed (m/s)
	1.5
running	
	6
a car	
	30
a plane	
sound	

Velocity

VELOCITY ([_____]) —
[_____] in a certain

[_____].

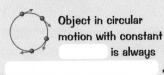 Object in circular
motion with constant
[_____] is always

[_____],

so object has [_____]

[_____].

Acceleration

ACCELERATION — the [_____]
in a certain amount of [_____].

acceleration
([___]) — $a = \dfrac{\Delta v}{t}$

change in
[_____] (m/s)

[_____] (s)

Deceleration is [_____]
(shows an object is [_____]).

Acceleration of object due to gravity close to
Earth's surface (object in [_____])
is roughly [_____].

 ☑ ☑ ☑

Topic 5 — Forces

Second Go: ..... /..... /.....	**Motion**

Distance and Displacement

DISTANCE (   ) —

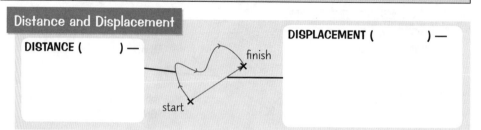

finish

start

DISPLACEMENT (   ) —

Speed

SPEED (   ) —

$s =$

People's   ,   and   speed can be affected by:

-
-
- distance travelled
-

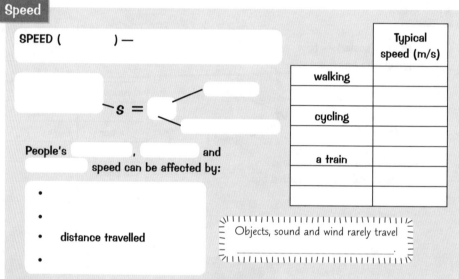

	Typical speed (m/s)
walking	
cycling	
a train	

Objects, sound and wind rarely travel
....

Velocity

VELOCITY (   ) —

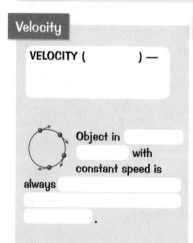

Object in   with constant speed is always

                .

Acceleration

ACCELERATION —

(m/s^2) \   / change in velocity (   )

—

Deceleration is

Acceleration of object due to gravity

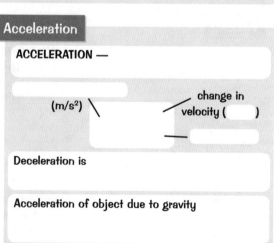

 ✓ ✓ ✓

Distance-Time & Velocity-Time Graphs

Distance-Time Graphs

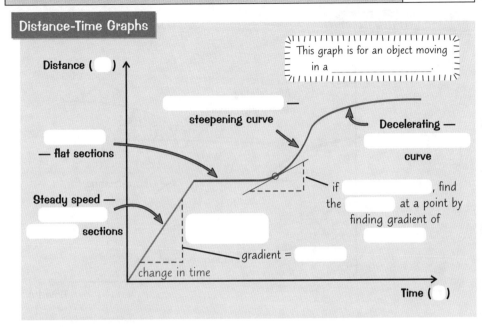

This graph is for an object moving in a _____.

Distance (   )

steepening curve

Decelerating — curve

— flat sections

Steady speed —

_____ sections

if _____, find the _____ at a point by finding gradient of

gradient =

change in time

Time (   )

Velocity-Time Graphs

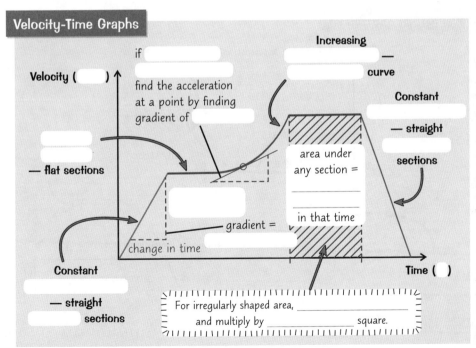

Velocity (   )

if _____ find the acceleration at a point by finding gradient of

Increasing _____ curve

Constant _____ — straight sections

— flat sections

area under any section = _____ _____ in that time

gradient =

change in time

Constant _____ — straight _____ sections

For irregularly shaped area, _____ and multiply by _____ square.

Topic 5 — Forces

Distance-Time & Velocity-Time Graphs

Distance-Time Graphs

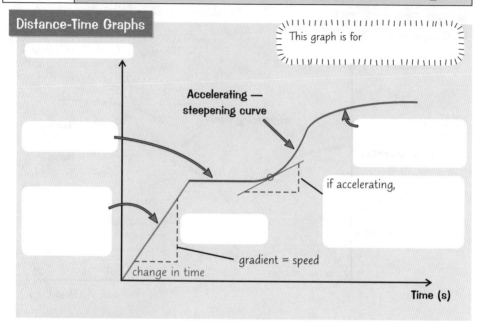

This graph is for

Accelerating —
steepening curve

if accelerating,

gradient = speed

change in time

Time (s)

Velocity-Time Graphs

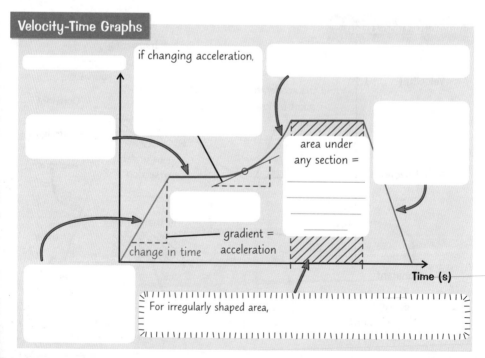

if changing acceleration,

area under
any section =

gradient =
acceleration

change in time

Time (s)

For irregularly shaped area,

Topic 5 — Forces

Newton's Laws of Motion

Newton's First Law

If [____] resultant force acts on stationary object, [_____].

If [____] resultant force acts on moving object, [_____]

[_____].

If [_____] resultant force acts on object, object [_____] (will change [____], [____]).

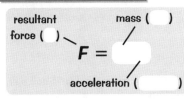

driving force ← → resistive force

INERTIA — the tendency of an object to continue in ....

Newton's Second Law

resultant force ([ ]) — mass ([ ])

$$F = \boxed{}$$

acceleration ([____])

- Acceleration is [_____] to resultant force — [____].
- Acceleration is [_____] to mass.

INERTIAL MASS — measure of [_____] it is to change an object's [_____]. It's the [_____] of force over acceleration: [____].

Same [____] applied to bowling ball and golf ball.

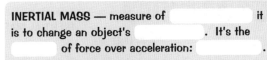
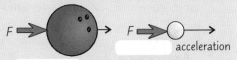

$F \rightarrow$ acceleration
acceleration

Bowling ball has bigger [_____], so it's harder to [_____] its [_____].

Newton's Third Law

Two interacting objects exert .... forces on each other.

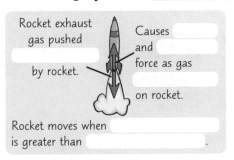

Rocket exhaust gas pushed [_____] by rocket.

Causes [____] and [____] force as gas [____] on rocket.

Rocket moves when [_____] is greater than [_____].

Girl [_____] on wall.

[____] — wall pushes back on girl with [____] and [____] force.

Second Go:
..... / ..... / .....

Newton's Laws of Motion

Newton's First Law

If zero resultant force acts on stationary object,

If zero resultant force acts on moving object,

force   force

If non-zero resultant force acts on object,

INERTIA —

Newton's Second Law

$$F = ma$$

mass (kg)

- **Acceleration is**

- **Acceleration is**

INERTIAL MASS —

Same   applied to bowling ball and golf ball.

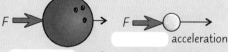

F   F

acceleration

acceleration

Bowling ball has bigger

Newton's Third Law

Rocket exhaust
gas pushed

Causes
and
            as gas
on rocket.

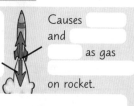

Two interacting objects

Girl pushes on wall.

Topic 5 — Forces

Mixed Practice Quizzes

Here's some quick-fire quiz questions covering p.79-84. Tick off each question you get right and then work out your quiz score to see how you're doing.

Quiz 1   Date: ...... / ...... / ......

1) What is inertia?

2) True or false? The speed of sound and the speed of wind are constant.

3) What is a typical walking speed?

4) True or false? According to Newton's Second Law, acceleration is inversely proportional to resultant force.

5) What is meant by the velocity of an object?

6) What units is acceleration measured in?

7) Describe how an object moving along a straight line at a steady speed would be represented on a distance-time graph.

8) Describe the difference between distance and displacement.

9) What does the gradient of a velocity-time graph tell you about an object?

10) What is Newton's Third Law?

Total:

Quiz 2   Date: ...... / ...... / ......

1) When a vehicle is travelling at a steady speed, is the driving force the same as or different to the resistive force?

2) What does a flat section of a velocity-time graph represent?

3) Give a typical speed for a car and a typical speed for a train.

4) What is meant by deceleration?

5) True or false? Moving objects often travel at a constant speed.

6) Describe how to find the speed of an object from a distance-time graph.

7) If a zero resultant force acts on a moving object, does the velocity of the object change or stay the same?

8) Give three factors that can affect a person's cycling speed.

9) What is inertial mass?

10) True or false? Velocity and speed are vector quantities.

Total:

Mixed Practice Quizzes

Quiz 3   Date: ...... / ...... / ......

1) What is Newton's First Law?

2) True or false? The acceleration of an object due to
   gravity close to the Earth's surface is roughly 12.8 m/s².

3) What does each symbol in $s = vt$ stand for?

4) What is a typical cycling speed?

5) Explain why an object moving in a circular motion
   with a constant speed has a changing velocity.

6) Describe how the speed of an object is changing when it is decelerating.

7) What does the gradient of a distance-time graph tell you about an object?

8) Define inertial mass as a ratio.

9) Describe how an object with a constant deceleration
   would be represented on a velocity-time graph.

10) Is distance a scalar or a vector quantity?

Total:

Quiz 4   Date: ...... / ...... / ......

1) What does a flat section of a distance-time graph represent?

2) What is a typical running speed?

3) What does the area under a section of a velocity-time graph tell you?

4) Give the equation for calculating acceleration, defining each symbol used.

5) True or false? The velocity of an object will only change
   if a non-zero resultant force acts on the object.

6) What is the speed of sound in air?

7) Give the equation for Newton's Second Law,
   defining each term used and their units.

8) Describe how an object accelerating along a straight line
   would be represented on a distance-time graph.

9) Give two factors that can affect a person's walking speed.

10) What does the gradient of a tangent of a distance-time graph tell you?

Total:

Terminal Velocity and Reaction Times

Terminal Velocity

FRICTION — a force that acts to

_____

_____ . It always acts

_____

_____ .

DRAG — the frictional force caused by any _____ on a _____ (e.g. _____).

Frictional forces from fluids always _____ .

Force of gravity _____ than frictional force.

↓

Object _____ .

↓

Speed _____ so friction _____ .

Frictional force _____ . → Resultant force is _____ . → _____ _____ reached.

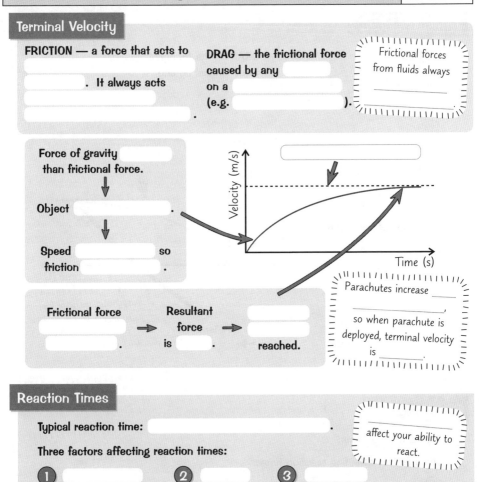

Velocity (m/s) / Time (s) graph

Parachutes increase _____ , so when parachute is deployed, terminal velocity is _____ .

Reaction Times

Typical reaction time: _____ .

Three factors affecting reaction times:

1 _____

2 _____

3 _____

_____ affect your ability to react.

The Ruler Drop Test

Three steps to investigate reaction time:

1 Get someone to hold _____ so _____ is between your _____ .

2 _____ dropped without _____ . _____ as _____ as possible.

3 Use _____ to _____ reaction time.

The _____ _____ , the longer the reaction time.

Terminal Velocity and Reaction Times

Second Go:
..... / ..... / .....

Terminal Velocity

FRICTION —

DRAG — the frictional force caused by any

Frictional forces

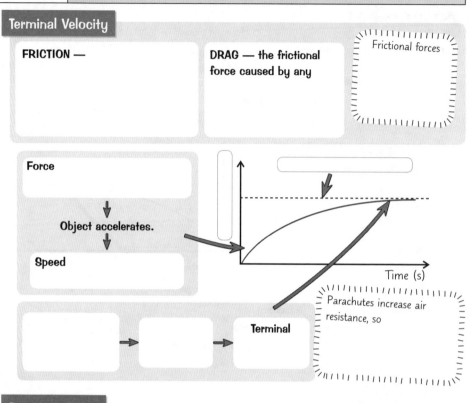

Force

↓

Object accelerates.

↓

Speed

Time (s)

→ → **Terminal**

Parachutes increase air resistance, so

Reaction Times

Typical reaction time: _____.

Three factors affecting reaction times:

1 _____ **2** _____ **3** _____

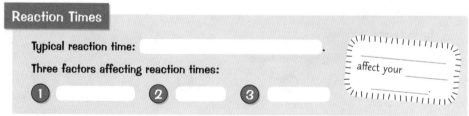

affect your _____

The Ruler Drop Test

Three steps to investigate reaction time:

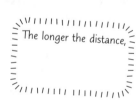

The longer the distance,

Stopping Distances

Stopping Distance Equation

Stopping distance = [   ] + [   ]

How far vehicle moves during ╱ [   ].

Distance taken to stop whilst [   ].

Two factors that increase thinking distance:

1 [   ]

2 slower driver [   ]

Four factors that increase braking distance:

1 faster vehicle

2 [   ] weather

3 poor road [   ]

4 damaged or worn [   ]

Stopping Distance Graphs

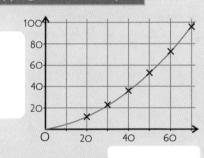

[   ]

100
80
60
40
20

O   20   40   60

[   ]

The bigger the _____ _____, the more _____ drivers need to leave between their car and the _____.

If speed doubles:

- Thinking distance [   ].

- Braking distance [   ].

Work Done When Stopping

Driver [   ], causing brake pads to be [   ] onto wheels.

[   ] between them causes [   ].

Energy [   ] from [   ] energy stores of wheels to [   ] energy stores of brakes.

Brakes [   ].

Large Decelerations

The [   ] a vehicle is going, the [   ] the [   ] needed to make it stop in a certain distance.

Larger braking force means larger [   ].

Very large deceleration can cause:

- brakes [   ]

- vehicle [   ]

Stopping Distances

Stopping Distance Equation

Stopping distance = Thinking Distance + Braking Distance

Two factors that increase thinking distance:

1
2

Four factors that increase braking distance:

1 faster vehicle speed
2
3
4

Stopping Distance Graphs

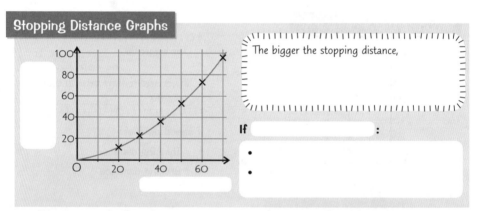

The bigger the stopping distance,

If   :

-
-

Work Done When Stopping

Driver brakes,

Friction

Energy

Brakes   .

Large Decelerations

The faster a vehicle is going,

Very large deceleration can cause:

-
-

Momentum

Calculating Momentum

momentum (_____)

$$p = mv$$

_____ (m/s)

_____

- The greater _____
  _____, the greater its
  momentum.
- The greater _____
  _____, the greater
  its momentum.

Conservation of Momentum

CONSERVATION OF MOMENTUM —
in a _____, total
momentum _____ an event
(e.g. a _____) _____
total momentum _____ an event.

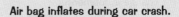

_____ explosion,
pieces fly off in different
directions so
momentum _____

_____
explosion,
momentum
is _____.

Forces, Momentum and Safety

The _____ acting on an object is equal to
its _____.

Increasing _____ for momentum to _____
_____ on object.

Five safety features that increase
time for change in momentum:

1. Air bags

2.

3.

4. Crash mats

5.

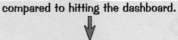

Air bag inflates during car crash.

Compressing air _____ your
_____ over a _____
compared to hitting the dashboard.

Rate of change of
momentum is _____.

Forces felt are _____
(meaning _____ injuries).

Topic 5 — Forces

Momentum

Calculating Momentum

$$p = \boxed{} \; \boxed{}$$

mass (kg)

-

-

Conservation of Momentum

CONSERVATION OF MOMENTUM —

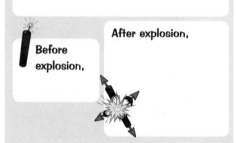

Before explosion,

After explosion,

Forces, Momentum and Safety

The resultant force acting on an object

Increasing time taken

Five safety features that increase time for change in momentum:

 1

 2

 3

 4

5

Compressing air

Forces

Mixed Practice Quizzes

Keep your revision momentum going by trying these quizzes covering p.87-92.

Quiz 1 Date: ...... / ...... / ......

1) Name four factors that increase the braking distance of a vehicle.

2) Give a typical human reaction time.

3) Describe the velocity-time graph for an object reaching a terminal velocity.

4) True or false? Frictional forces from fluids always decrease with speed.

5) Describe the work done by a vehicle when its brakes are applied.

6) Give the formula for calculating momentum.

7) True or false? Distractions can affect your ability to react.

8) What is meant by conservation of momentum?

9) Seat belts reduce injuries by increasing the time taken for a change in momentum. Name two other safety features that work in this way.

10) Name three factors that affect reaction times.

Total:

Quiz 2 Date: ...... / ...... / ......

1) True or false? Cycle helmets reduce the time for a change in momentum.

2) The stopping distance of a vehicle is the sum of the thinking distance and what other distance?

3) What causes an object dropped from a height to accelerate?

4) Two objects are travelling at the same velocity. One has a larger mass and the other has a smaller mass. Which object will have a larger momentum?

5) True or false? The greater the speed of a vehicle, the greater its stopping distance.

6) What is friction?

7) If a vehicle's speed doubles, does the thinking distance double or halve?

8) Give two negative effects caused by the large deceleration of a vehicle.

9) What are the units of momentum?

10) If a person with a slow reaction time does the ruler drop test, will the ruler fall a short way or a long way before they catch it?

Total:

Topic 5 — Forces

Mixed Practice Quizzes

Quiz 3 — Date: ...... / ...... / ......

1) Why would slower driver reaction times increase the stopping distance of a car?

2) Explain how a falling object eventually reaches a terminal velocity.

3) True or false? A larger braking force means a larger deceleration.

4) Describe an experiment you could do to investigate someone's reaction time.

5) What is meant by the braking distance of a vehicle?

6) Does the friction acting on an object work in the same direction or the opposite direction to its movement?

7) Which energy store is energy transferred to when a car brakes?

8) As the velocity of an object increases, what happens to its momentum?

9) True or false? The faster a vehicle is going, the greater the braking force needed to stop it in a certain distance.

10) Give two factors that increase thinking distance.

Total:

Quiz 4 — Date: ...... / ...... / ......

1) True or false? The resultant force acting on an object is equal to its rate of change in momentum.

2) What is the resultant force acting on a falling object when it reaches its terminal velocity?

3) Name one other factor, apart from tiredness, that can affect reaction time.

4) What is meant by the thinking distance?

5) Explain why the brakes heat up when a vehicle is braking.

6) What is drag?

7) Why can large decelerations be dangerous?

8) Explain how momentum is conserved in an explosion.

9) Describe how air bags can reduce injuries in a car crash.

10) True or false? If a vehicle's speed doubles, its braking distance quadruples.

Total:

Transverse and Longitudinal Waves

Wave Basics

When waves travel through a medium, they [____] [____].

Sound waves move away...

...

Ripples on water's surface move away...

...

FREQUENCY — number of [____] [____] passing a certain point [____].

PERIOD — amount of time it takes for a [____] [____].

AMPLITUDE — [____] of a point on a wave from [____].

Displacement

Distance (m)

WAVELENGTH — length of [____].

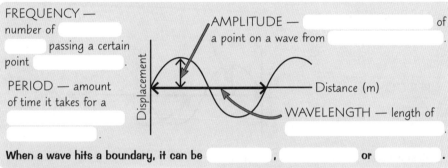

When a wave hits a boundary, it can be [____], [____] or [____].

Transverse Waves

Oscillations perpendicular ([____]) to direction of [____].

Three types of transverse waves:

1 [____] in water

2 Electromagnetic waves (e.g. [____])

3 Waves [____]

Longitudinal Waves

Oscillations [____] to direction of [____].

[____]

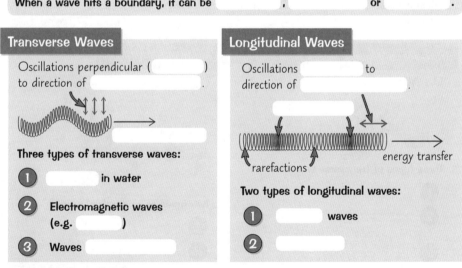

rarefactions

energy transfer

Two types of longitudinal waves:

1 [____] waves

2 [____]

The Wave Equation

WAVE SPEED — speed at which a [____] [____] (or speed [____] [____]).

1 Hz is [____].

frequency ([____], Hz)

wave speed ([____]) —— $v = $ [____] λ [____] (m)

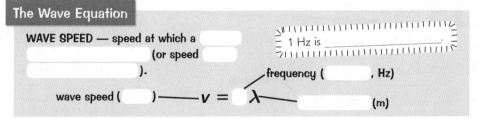

 ☑ ☑   ☑

Transverse and Longitudinal Waves

Wave Basics

When waves travel

Sound waves [ ] ...

Ripples [ ]

...

...   .

FREQUENCY —

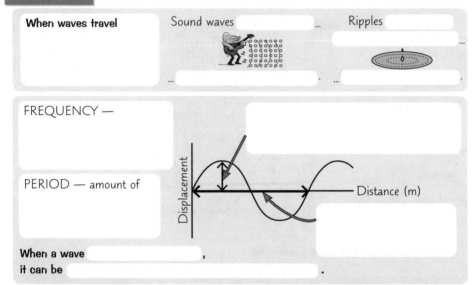

PERIOD — amount of

Displacement

Distance (m)

When a wave [ ],
it can be [ ].

Transverse Waves

Oscillations [ ]
to [ ].

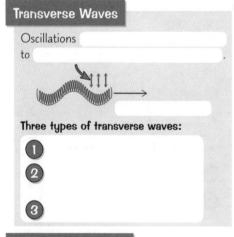

Three types of transverse waves:

1
2
3

Longitudinal Waves

Oscillations [ ] to [ ].

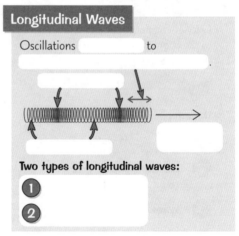

Two types of longitudinal waves:

1
2

The Wave Equation

WAVE SPEED —

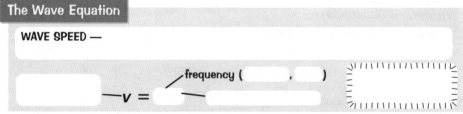

frequency (,)

$v =$

 ☑ ☑ ☑

Speed of Sound and Reflection

Measuring the Speed of Sound

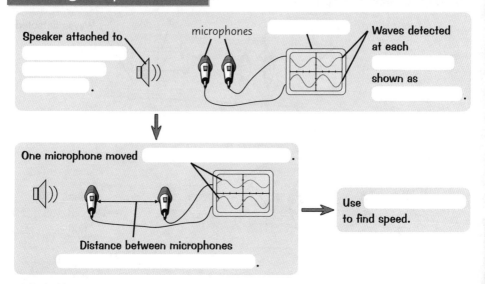

Speaker attached to
_____
_____ .

microphones _____

Waves detected at each _____

shown as _____

One microphone moved _____ .

Distance between microphones
_____ .

Use _____ to find speed.

Reflection

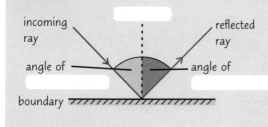

incoming ray

reflected ray

angle of _____

angle of _____

boundary

Angle of incidence always _____ .

Diffuse Reflection

reflected rays _____
_____ .

incoming rays

surface

Surface appears _____ (e.g. piece of paper).

Specular Reflection

reflected rays _____
_____ .

incoming rays

surface

Surface gives clear reflection (e.g. _____).

Topic 6 — Waves

98

Second Go:
..... /..... /.....

Speed of Sound and Reflection

Measuring the Speed of Sound

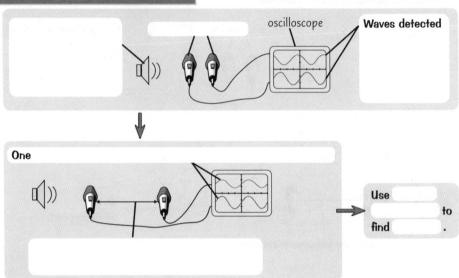

oscilloscope

Waves detected

One

Use [ ] to find [ ].

Reflection

ray

normal

ray

boundary

always

Diffuse Reflection

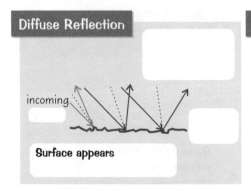

incoming

Surface appears

Specular Reflection

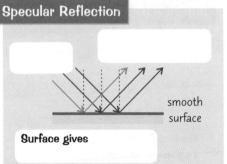

smooth surface

Surface gives

Refraction and EM Waves

Refraction

REFRACTION — when a wave _____ as it crosses a boundary between _____ .

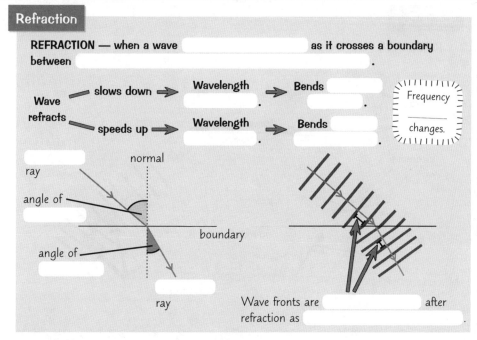

Wave refracts — slows down ➡ Wavelength ➡ _____ Bends _____ .

Wave refracts — speeds up ➡ Wavelength ➡ _____ Bends _____ .

Frequency _____ changes.

_____ ray

angle of _____

normal

boundary

angle of _____

_____ ray

Wave fronts are _____ after refraction as _____ .

The Electromagnetic (EM) Spectrum

The EM spectrum is _____ .

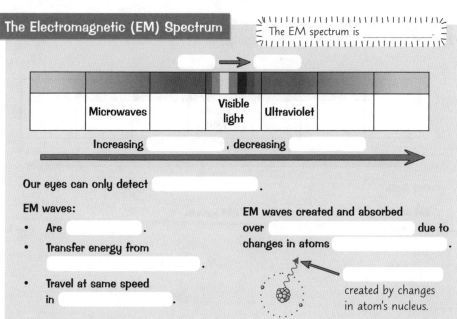

	Microwaves		Visible light	Ultraviolet		

Increasing _____ , decreasing _____

Our eyes can only detect _____ .

EM waves:

• Are _____ .

• Transfer energy from _____

• Travel at same speed in _____ .

EM waves created and absorbed over _____ due to changes in atoms _____ .

_____ created by changes in atom's nucleus.

Refraction and EM Waves

Refraction

REFRACTION —

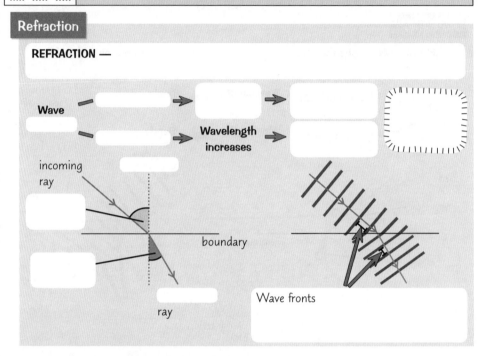

Wave

Wavelength increases

incoming ray

boundary

ray

Wave fronts

The Electromagnetic (EM) Spectrum

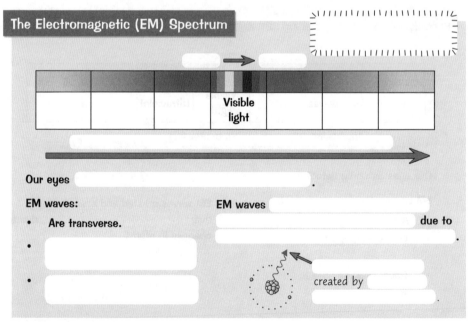

Visible light

Our eyes

EM waves:

• Are transverse.

•

•

EM waves

due to

created by

 ☑ ☑ ☑

Uses and Dangers of EM Waves

Producing Radio Waves

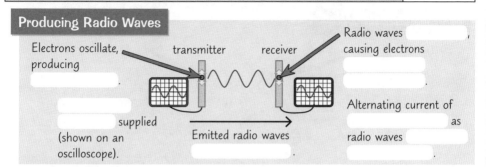

Electrons oscillate, producing [____].

[____] supplied (shown on an oscilloscope).

transmitter   receiver

Emitted radio waves [____].

Radio waves [____], causing electrons [____].

Alternating current of [____] as radio waves [____].

Uses of EM Waves

Radio waves
- TV
- [____]

Microwaves
- Satellite
- [____]

Infrared radiation
- [____]
- [____]
- Infrared [____]

Visible light
- Communications through [____]

UV waves
- Energy efficient [____]

X-rays and gamma rays
- Medical [____]
- [____]

Dangers of EM Waves

RADIATION DOSE — measure of the [____] to body tissues due to [____]. It is measured in sieverts.

Risk depends on:
- [____] of dose
- Type [____]

1 sievert ([____]) = [____] millisieverts (mSv).

Type of ionising radiation	UV	X-rays and [____]
Harmful effects on human body tissue	• Can prematurely [____] • Increases risk of [____]	• [____] • Cancer

Second Go:
...../...../.....

Uses and Dangers of EM Waves

Producing Radio Waves

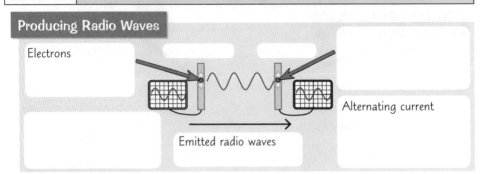

Electrons

Alternating current

Emitted radio waves

Uses of EM Waves

Radio waves
-
- Radio

Microwaves
-
-

Infrared radiation
-
-
-

Visible light
-

UV waves
-
-

X-rays and gamma rays
- Medical imaging
-

Dangers of EM Waves

RADIATION DOSE — measure of _____
_____. **It is measured in sieverts.**

Risk depends on:
-
-

1 sievert (Sv) =

Type of ionising radiation	UV	X-rays and gamma rays
Harmful effects on human body tissue	• •	• •

 ☑ ☑ ☑

Mixed Practice Quizzes

Time to reflect on the what you've learnt so far by doing some questions covering p.95-102. Tick off each question you get right to keep track of your progress.

Quiz 1   Date: ...... / ...... / ......

1) What type of EM wave has the longest wavelength? ☑

2) How many sieverts are equal to 1000 millisieverts? ☑

3) Is it transverse waves or longitudinal waves that have oscillations perpendicular to the direction of energy transfer? ☑

4) Give the formula for calculating wave speed, defining each term used. ☑

5) True or false? All EM waves travel at the same speed in a vacuum. ☑

6) Are electromagnetic waves transverse or longitudinal? ☑

7) True or false? Microwaves can be used in sun tan beds. ☑

8) Describe the difference between diffuse reflection and specular reflection. ☑

9) A wave can be reflected when it hits a boundary.
State two other things that can happen to a wave when it hits a boundary. ☑

10) True or false? An alternating current can be used to generate radio waves. ☑

Total: ☐

Quiz 2   Date: ...... / ...... / ......

1) Define: a) the 'period' of a wave, b) the 'frequency' of a wave. ☑

2) A wave refracts at a boundary and speeds up.
State how its wavelength changes. ☑

3) True or false? Transverse waves have compressions and rarefactions. ☑

4) What type of surface reflects rays in only one direction? ☑

5) What type of EM wave has the lowest frequency? ☑

6) True or false? Gamma rays can be made by changes in an atom's nucleus. ☑

7) What can microwaves and infrared radiation both be used for? ☑

8) True or false? The angle of incidence always equals the angle of reflection when a ray is reflected at a boundary. ☑

9) What are the units of frequency? ☑

10) Give one use of X-rays and gamma rays. ☑

Total: ☐

Mixed Practice Quizzes

Date: ...... / ...... / ......

1) True or false? The EM spectrum is continuous.

2) Give one example of a transverse wave and one example of a longitudinal wave.

3) Give one example of an object that displays specular reflection.

4) What does the ray diagram look like for the refraction of a wave that decreases in speed as it hits a boundary?

5) True or false? Waves transfer energy and matter.

6) What type of EM wave lies between radio waves and infrared on the EM spectrum?

7) How are radio waves produced?

8) Define: a) the 'amplitude' of a wave, b) the 'wavelength' of a wave.

9) Give two harmful effects of exposure to X-rays and gamma rays.

10) What is refraction?

Total:

Quiz 4   Date: ...... / ...... / ......

1) Give two harmful effects of exposure to UV radiation.

2) Define wave speed.

3) True or false? Ripples on a water's surface carry the water away.

4) What type of surface causes diffuse reflection?

5) True or false? EM waves transfer energy from absorber to source.

6) Describe an experiment you could do to measure the speed of sound in air.

7) Describe the difference between transverse and longitudinal waves.

8) True or false? Changes in atoms and their nuclei causes EM waves to be created or absorbed over a large frequency range.

9) What does radiation dose measure?

10) Between radio waves and gamma rays, which has:
   a) the shortest frequency? b) the shortest wavelength?

Total:

Lenses and Magnification

Images

REAL IMAGE	image formed when light rays from a point on an object
VIRTUAL IMAGE	image formed when light rays but have actually come from another

Lenses form images by ....

Convex Lenses

Convex lenses can produce _____ .

_____ rays

F ------ axis

Principal focus — point where _____

_____ — distance between _____ and principal focus.

_____ come together.

Concave Lenses

Concave lenses always produce _____ .

_____

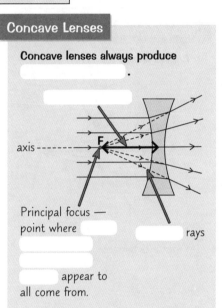

axis -----

Principal focus — point where _____ _____ rays

_____ appear to all come from.

Magnifying Glasses

Magnifying glasses use _____ to create a _____ .

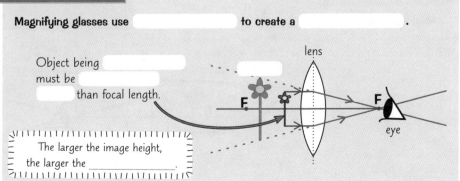

Object being _____ must be _____ than focal length.

lens

F

F

eye

The larger the image height, the larger the ....

Lenses and Magnification

Images

REAL IMAGE	
VIRTUAL IMAGE	

Lenses form images by

Convex Lenses

Convex lenses

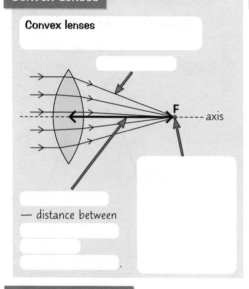

axis

— distance between

Concave Lenses

Concave lenses

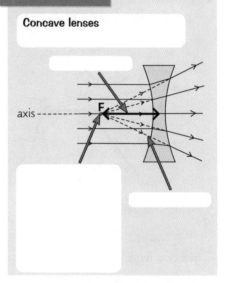

axis

Magnifying Glasses

Magnifying glasses ....**.**

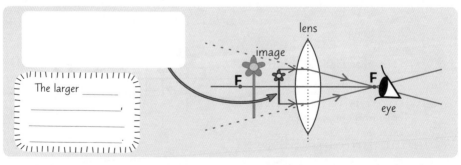

The larger ....
....
..................'

lens

image

F

F

eye

Topic 6 — Waves

 ☑ ☑ ☑

Ray Diagrams

Four Ray Diagrams for Convex Lenses

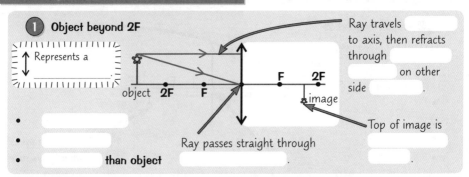

1 Object beyond 2F

Represents a
....

object 2F F F 2F image

Ray travels _____
to axis, then refracts
through _____
_____ on other
side _____

Ray passes straight through _____

Top of image is _____

• _____
• _____
• _____ than object

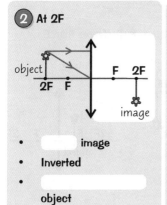

2 At 2F

object 2F F F 2F image

• _____ image
• Inverted
• _____ object

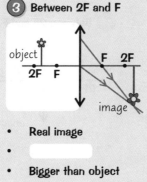

3 Between 2F and F

object 2F F F 2F image

• Real image
• _____
• Bigger than object

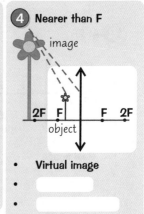

4 Nearer than F

image 2F F object F 2F

• Virtual image
• _____
• _____ object

Ray Diagram for Concave Lenses

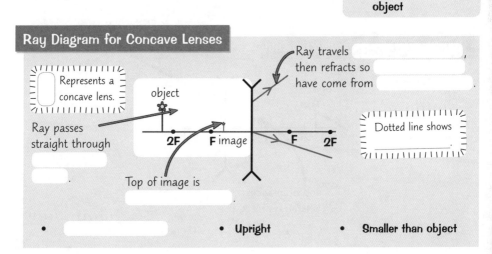

Represents a
concave lens.

Ray travels _____
then refracts so _____,
have come from _____

object 2F F image F 2F

Ray passes
straight through
_____ .

Top of image is
_____

Dotted line shows
....

• _____
• Upright
• Smaller than object

Ray Diagrams

Four Ray Diagrams for Convex Lenses

1 Object beyond 2F

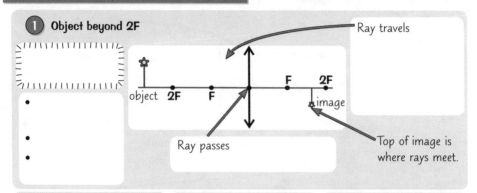

Ray travels

Ray passes

Top of image is where rays meet.

2 At 2F

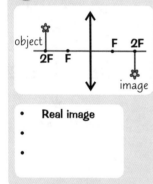

- **Real image**
-
-

3 Between 2F and F

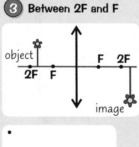

-
-
-

4 Nearer than F

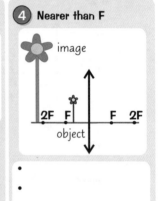

-
-

Ray Diagram for Concave Lenses

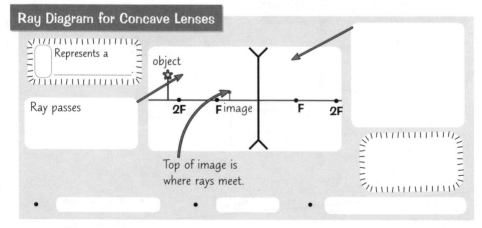

Represents a
....

Ray passes

Top of image is where rays meet.

-
-
-

Visible Light

Colour

In the visible light [ ], every colour has a [ ] (and frequencies).

White light is made up of _____.

- Opaque objects [ ].

- Colour depends on [ ] that are most reflected.

All other wavelengths are _____.

red apple

Black objects [ ] wavelengths of visible light.

White objects [ ] wavelengths of visible light [ ].

- Transparent ([ ]) or translucent ([ ]) objects transmit light.

- Colour depends on wavelengths of light it [ ].

white

Colour Filters

Colour filters transmit [ ] and absorb the rest.

Red hat

Reflects [ ].

Viewed through:
Green filter
OR
Blue filter

→ [ ] light. → Hat appears [ ]

Viewed through: Red filter

→ [ ] light. → Hat appears [ ]

| Second Go: ...../...../..... | **Visible Light** |

Colour

In the visible light spectrum, [ ]

[ ]

[ ].

_____ is made up of _____.

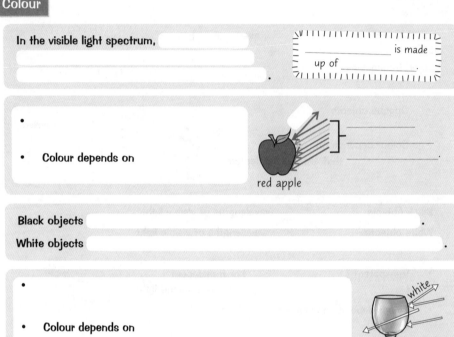

- [ ]

- Colour depends on

_____
_____
_____.

red apple

Black objects [ ].

White objects [ ].

- [ ]

- Colour depends on

white

Colour Filters

[ ]

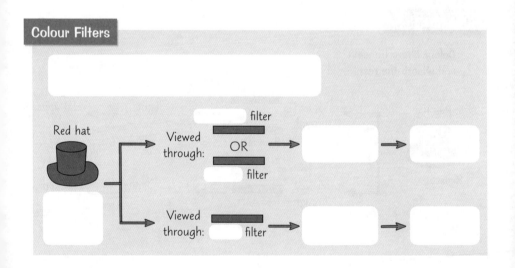

Red hat

Viewed through: [ ] filter OR [ ] filter → [ ] → [ ]

Viewed through: [ ] filter → [ ] → [ ]

Mixed Practice Quizzes

Bring your physics knowledge to light with some quiz questions on p.105-110.

Quiz 1   Date: ...... / ...... / ......

1) What colour filter would a green object need to be viewed through to appear green?

2) What symbol represents a concave lens on a ray diagram?

3) Describe the difference in shape between a convex and a concave lens.

4) What type of lens do magnifying glasses use?

5) If an opaque object is yellow, is it reflecting or absorbing yellow light?

6) True or false? An object at 2F will produce a real, inverted image the same size as the object when viewed through a convex lens.

7) True or false? White objects absorb all wavelengths of visible light.

8) What is meant by a 'real image'?

9) Which type of lens brings together light rays that travel parallel to its axis?

10) Which can transmit light — opaque objects or translucent objects?

Total:

Quiz 2   Date: ...... / ...... / ......

1) What is meant by the 'principal focus' of a convex lens?

2) True or false? Opaque objects transmit light.

3) Describe the image formed by an object viewed through a concave lens.

4) What does the ray diagram look like for an object viewed through a convex lens when the object is further than 2F from the lens?

5) What does the colour of an opaque object depend on?

6) True or false? Lenses form objects by refracting light.

7) At what distance does an object have to be from a convex lens to make a virtual, upright image that is bigger than the object?

8) Do magnifying glasses create real images or virtual images?

9) What do transparent and translucent objects both have in common?

10) If an opaque object appears red, does it reflect or absorb blue wavelengths of light?

Total:

Mixed Practice Quizzes

Quiz 3 Date: ...... / ...... / ......

1) If a red object is viewed through a blue filter, what colour will it appear?
2) What is the name for the length between a lens and its principal focus?
3) True or false? Convex lenses always produce virtual images.
4) Describe the image formed when an object placed somewhere between F and 2F away from a convex lens is viewed through the lens.
5) If an opaque object reflects all the wavelengths of visible light equally, what colour will it be?
6) True or false? Black objects don't absorb any wavelengths of visible light.
7) Do lenses form images by reflecting or refracting light?
8) What do colour filters do?
9) What is meant by a 'virtual image'?
10) What does the ray diagram look like for an object viewed through a concave lens when the object is further than 2F from the lens?

Total:

Quiz 4 Date: ...... / ...... / ......

1) What does the colour of a translucent object depend on?
2) What is meant by the 'focal length' of a lens?
3) Do concave lenses produce real images, virtual images or both?
4) True or false? For any magnifying glass, the larger the image height, the larger the magnification.
5) Which type of lens makes light rays travelling parallel to its axis appear to all come from the same point?
6) True or false? In the visible light spectrum, each colour has a small range of wavelengths.
7) What do dotted lines on ray diagrams represent?
8) In terms of the reflection and absorption of visible light, describe the difference between black objects and white objects.
9) Why does a red object appear black when viewed through a green filter?
10) What symbol represents a convex lens on a ray diagram?

Total:

Emitting and Absorbing Radiation

Infrared Radiation

All objects continually [____] infrared (IR) radiation.

The higher an object's temperature, _____ in a certain amount of time.

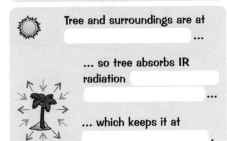

Tree and surroundings are at [____] ...

... so tree absorbs IR radiation [____] ...

... which keeps it at [____] .

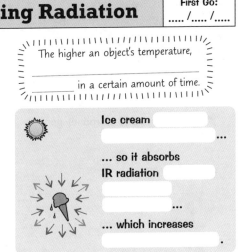

Ice cream [____] ...

... so it absorbs IR radiation [____] ...

... which increases [____]

Black Bodies

PERFECT BLACK BODY — an object that [____] .

Two properties of perfect black bodies:

1. Best possible [____]

2. Don't [____] or [____] any radiation.

Intensity

As object gets hotter, intensity of [____] [____] and peak wavelength [____] .

Wavelength

Radiation and Earth's Temperature

Daytime: Earth .... more radiation than it ....

↓

Local temperature ....

Nighttime: Earth .... more radiation than it ....

↓

Local temperature ....

Overall, temperature of Earth _____

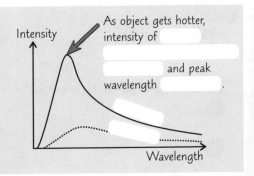

Radiation emitted by [____] , and [____] .

Some radiation

Space

Atmosphere

Earth's surface

Some radiation from Sun [____] , clouds and [____]

 ☑ ☑ ☑

Emitting and Absorbing Radiation

Infrared Radiation

All objects [_____]
[_____]

The higher _____,
in a _____ .

	Tree and surroundings ...			Ice cream ...
	... so ...			... so ...
	... which			... which

Black Bodies

PERFECT BLACK BODY — [_____]

Two properties of perfect black bodies:

1 [_____]

2 [_____]

As object gets hotter,

Wavelength

Radiation and Earth's Temperature

Daytime: [_____]

↓

Local temperature [_____]

Nighttime: [_____]

↓

Local temperature [_____]

Overall, _____
_____ .

Some radiation reflected

Space

Atmosphere

Earth's surface

Some radiation [_____]

Sound Waves

Vibrations

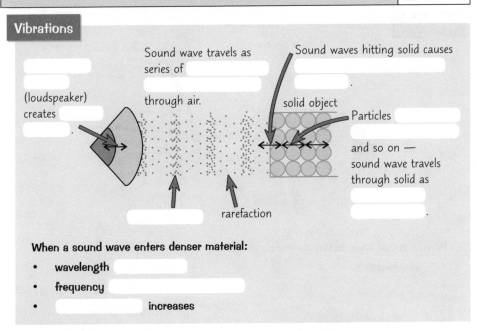

Sound wave travels as series of [____] through air.

Sound waves hitting solid causes [____].

(loudspeaker) creates [____].

solid object

Particles [____]

and so on — sound wave travels through solid as [____].

rarefaction

When a sound wave enters denser material:

- wavelength [____]
- frequency [____]
- [____] increases

Hearing Sound

Sound waves [____].

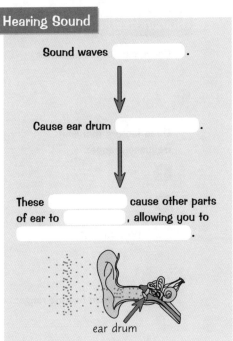

Cause ear drum [____].

These [____] cause other parts of ear to [____], allowing you to [____].

ear drum

Human Hearing

Conversion of sound waves to [____] at [____] only works over a [____].

Three factors that limit frequency range:

1. Size of [____].
2. [____] of ear drum.
3. Structure of [____] that vibrate.

Normal human hearing range:
20 Hz – ....

Sound Waves

Vibrations

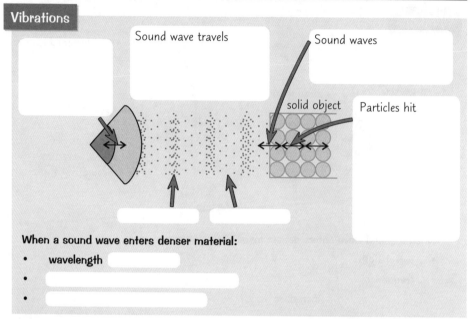

Sound wave travels

Sound waves

solid object

Particles hit

When a sound wave enters denser material:

- wavelength

-

-

Hearing Sound

Sound waves

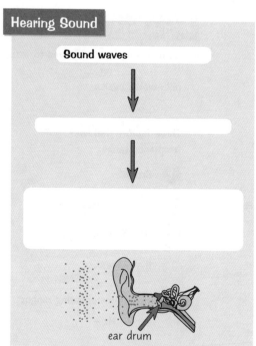

ear drum

Human Hearing

Conversion of sound waves

Three factors that limit frequency range:

1

2

3 Structure of

Normal human hearing range:

.... – ....

Uses of Sound Waves

Ultrasound

ULTRASOUND — sound waves with frequencies [   ].

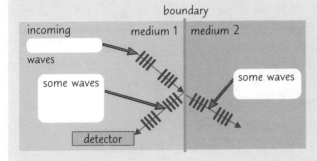

boundary

incoming [   ] waves

medium 1 | medium 2

some waves

some waves

detector

Time it takes ultrasound waves to be [   ] [   ] from boundary and [   ] can be used to measure [   ].

Three uses of ultrasound:

1. Medical imaging, e.g. [   ].

2. [   ], e.g. finding flaws in materials.

3. Echo sounding, e.g. finding depth of water or [   ].

Seismic Waves

Earthquakes produce [   ].
Detecting seismic waves gives evidence for [   ] and [   ].

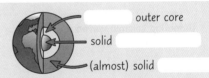

[   ] outer core

solid [   ]

(almost) solid [   ]

P-waves

- [   ] waves.
- Travel through [   ].

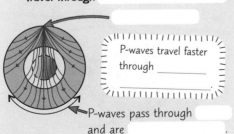

[   ]

P-waves travel faster through _____

P-waves pass through [   ] and are [   ].

S-waves

- [   ] waves.
- Can't travel through [   ].

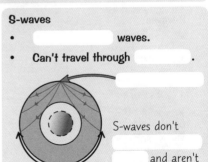

[   ]

S-waves don't [   ] and aren't [   ].

118

Uses of Sound Waves

Ultrasound

ULTRASOUND —

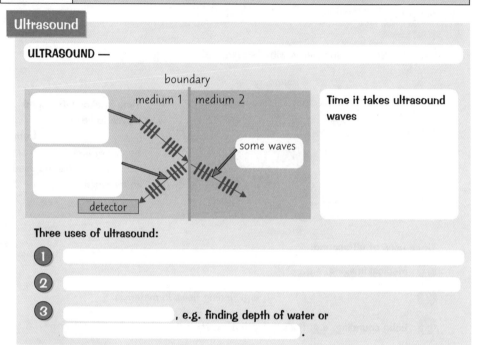

boundary

medium 1   medium 2

some waves

detector

Time it takes ultrasound waves

Three uses of ultrasound:

1.

2.

3. _____ , e.g. finding depth of water or _____ .

Seismic Waves

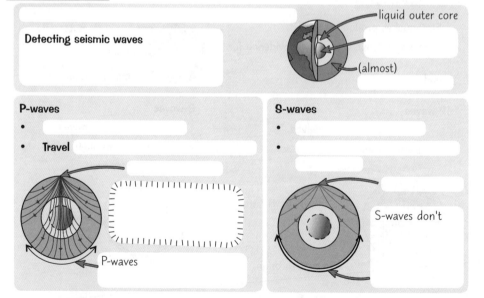

Detecting seismic waves

liquid outer core

(almost)

P-waves
-
- Travel

P-waves

S-waves
-
-

S-waves don't

Topic 6 — Waves

Mixed Practice Quizzes

Wave goodbye to Topic 6 with these quiz questions, which cover p.113-118.

Quiz 1 — Date: ...... / ...... / ......

1) What event causes seismic waves to be produced?
2) What is the normal range of human hearing?
3) True or false? P-waves can travel through both solids and liquids.
4) What is a perfect black body?
5) What happens when ultrasound waves meet a boundary between two different media?
6) Explain why the Earth's local temperature increases during the day.
7) Describe how sound waves travel through a solid.
8) Ultrasound can be used for medical imaging. What else can ultrasound be used for?
9) Name two types of seismic wave.
10) True or false? The ear drum vibrates when sound waves hit it.

Total:

Quiz 2 — Date: ...... / ...... / ......

1) Define ultrasound.
2) What type of object absorbs all the radiation that hits it?
3) If a sound wave passes from air to a solid, does its wave speed change or stay the same?
4) In terms of the emission and absorption of radiation, explain why the local temperature of the Earth changes between day and night.
5) Give one factor that limits the frequency range over which sound waves are converted to vibrations in the ear drum.
6) True or false? P-waves are transverse waves.
7) What is the highest frequency of sound that a human ear can detect?
8) What can echo sounding be used for?
9) If an object's temperature rises, will it then emit more or less IR radiation?
10) True or false? A perfect black body is the best possible emitter of radiation.

Total:

Mixed Practice Quizzes

Quiz 3   Date: ...... / ...... / ......

1) Are S-waves longitudinal or transverse?

2) If an object is at a lower temperature than its surroundings, explain why its temperature increases in terms of the rate it absorbs and emits radiation.

3) What is the name for sound waves with frequencies higher than 20 kHz?

4) True or false? Perfect black bodies don't transmit or absorb any radiation.

5) What happens to the particles in a solid when a sound wave hits the solid?

6) Explain why the Earth's local temperature decreases at nighttime.

7) Why can humans only hear sound waves in a certain frequency range?

8) True or false? The hotter an object, the more IR radiation it radiates in a certain amount of time.

9) Do P-waves travel through solids and liquids at the same speed or different speeds?

10) Give one use of ultrasound.

Total:

Quiz 4   Date: ...... / ...... / ......

1) Can human ears detect ultrasound?

2) True or false? Sound waves can cause vibrations in solids.

3) How can ultrasound waves be used to find the distance between a boundary and a detector?

4) True or false? All objects continually emit and absorb infrared radiation.

5) What do P- and S-waves provide evidence for?

6) State two ways that clouds prevent radiation from the Sun reaching the Earth's surface.

7) When sound waves reach your ear, what enables you to hear sound?

8) True or false? S-waves can't travel through liquids.

9) If an object is at the same temperature as its surroundings, explain why it stays at that temperature in terms of the rate it absorbs and emits radiation.

10) What type of object doesn't reflect or transmit any radiation?

Total:

Magnets

First Go:
..... /..... /.....

Magnetic Fields

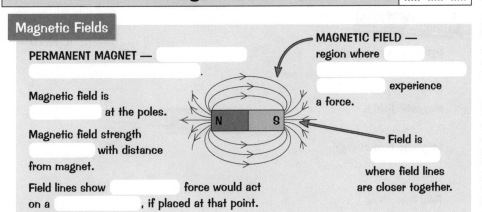

PERMANENT MAGNET — [   ]
[   ].

Magnetic field is
[   ] at the poles.

Magnetic field strength
[   ] with distance
from magnet.

Field lines show [   ] force would act
on a [   ], if placed at that point.

MAGNETIC FIELD —
region where [   ]
[   ] experience
a force.

Field is
[   ]
where field lines
are closer together.

Repulsion

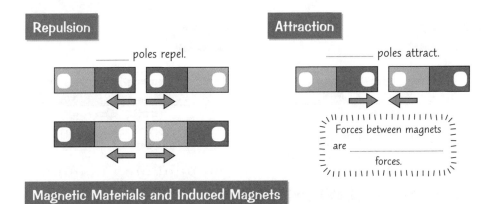

.... poles repel.

Attraction

.... poles attract.

Forces between magnets
are ....
forces.

Magnetic Materials and Induced Magnets

INDUCED MAGNET — a [   ] that turns
into a magnet when it's put in [   ].

Four magnetic materials:

1. iron
2. [   ]
3. nickel
4. [   ]

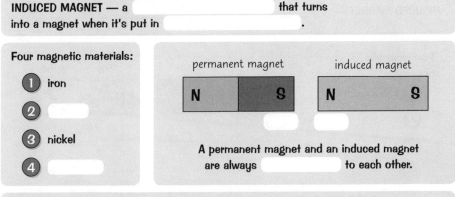

permanent magnet

N   S

induced magnet

N   S

A permanent magnet and an induced magnet
are always [   ] to each other.

When the induced magnet is moved away from the permanent magnet,
it [   ].

Magnets

Magnetic Fields

PERMANENT MAGNET —

Magnetic field is

Magnetic field strength

Field lines show

MAGNETIC FIELD —

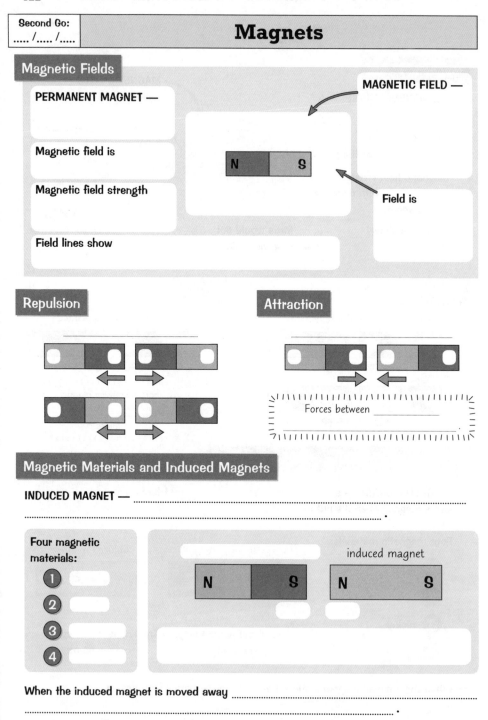

Field is

Repulsion

Attraction

Forces between

Magnetic Materials and Induced Magnets

INDUCED MAGNET — ....
....

Four magnetic
materials:

1

2

3

4

induced magnet

N   S   N   S

When the induced magnet is moved away ....
....

Topic 7 — Magnetism and Electromagnetism

Compasses and Electromagnetism

Compasses

Compass needle points in the direction of

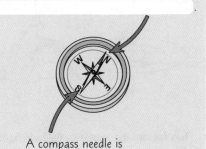

A compass needle is

When a compass isn't near a magnet, its needle points to line up with the Earth's

Current-Carrying Wire

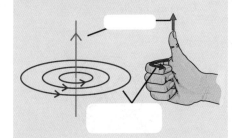

Two factors the magnetic field strength depends on:

1 Size of

2 the wire.

Solenoids and Magnetic Fields

Twisting a wire into a solenoid the magnetic field strength around the wire.

Magnetic fields of each turn of wire

So magnetic field inside solenoid is

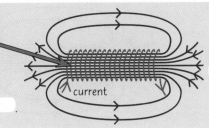
current

magnetic field (same shape as a)

ELECTROMAGNET — a solenoid with an . It is a magnet that can be

Putting an increases

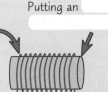

Electromagnets are used in and in scrap yards to

Topic 7 — Magnetism and Electromagnetism

Second Go:
..... /..... /.....

Compasses and Electromagnetism

Compasses

Compass needle

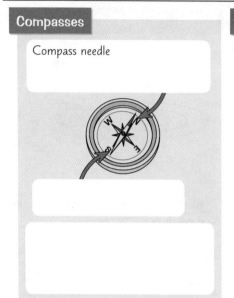

Current-Carrying Wire

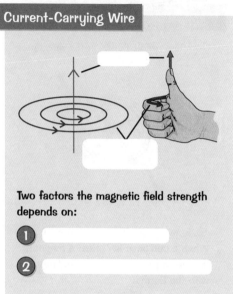

Two factors the magnetic field strength depends on:

1

2

Solenoids and Magnetic Fields

Twisting a wire into a solenoid ....

....

Magnetic fields of

So magnetic field

current

magnetic field

ELECTROMAGNET —

Putting an

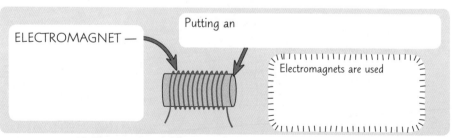

Electromagnets are used

Topic 7 — Magnetism and Electromagnetism

The Motor Effect

Force on a Conductor

MOTOR EFFECT — when a magnet and conductor exert [____].

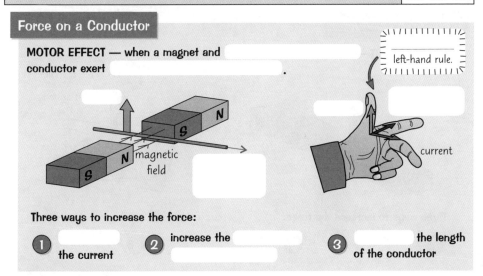

left-hand rule.

magnetic field

current

Three ways to increase the force:

1 [____] the current

2 increase the [____]

3 [____] the length of the conductor

Electric Motors

[____] is passed through wire.

↓

Each side of the coil [____]

↓

Coil rotates.

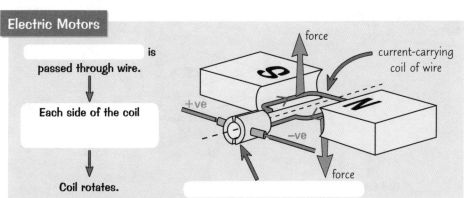

force

current-carrying coil of wire

+ve

S

N

−ve

force

Loudspeakers and Headphones

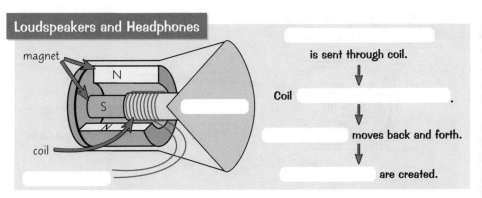

magnet

N

S

coil

[____] is sent through coil.

↓

Coil [____].

↓

[____] moves back and forth.

↓

[____] are created.

Topic 7 — Magnetism and Electromagnetism

The Motor Effect

Force on a Conductor

MOTOR EFFECT —

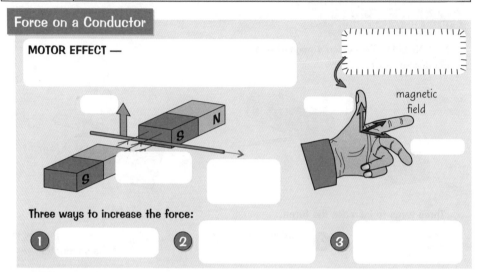

magnetic field

Three ways to increase the force:

1️⃣ ⬜   2️⃣ ⬜   3️⃣ ⬜

Electric Motors

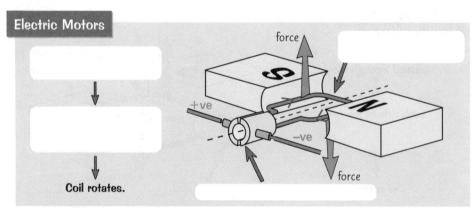

force

+ve

−ve

force

Coil rotates.

Loudspeakers and Headphones

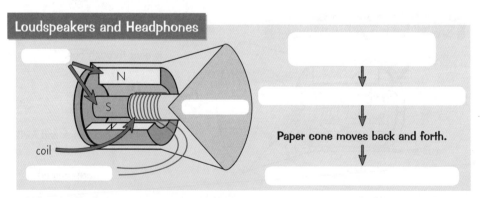

N

S

N

coil

Paper cone moves back and forth.

The Generator Effect & Microphones

The Generator Effect

GENERATOR EFFECT — when a ⬚
is induced in a wire which is moving relative to a magnetic field,
or experiencing a ⬚ .

If the wire's in a
complete ⬚

Two ways to induce a ⬚ ...	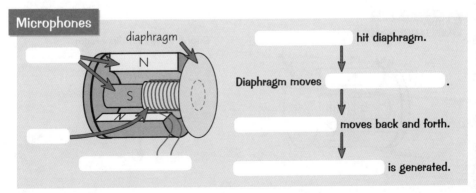	Move the wire.
To swap the direction of the ⬚ ...	Move the magnet in ⬚ . **or** Start with the magnet ⬚	Move the wire in ⬚ . **or** Start with both magnets the ⬚
To increase the size of the induced ⬚ ...	Increase the ⬚ . **or** Increase the ⬚ .	

An induced current generates its own ⬚ .
An induced current generates a ⬚ that
always ⬚ the change that made it.

Microphones

diaphragm

⬚ hit diaphragm.

Diaphragm moves ⬚ .

⬚ moves back and forth.

⬚ is generated.

The Generator Effect & Microphones

The Generator Effect

GENERATOR EFFECT — ....

....

....

....

	①	②
Two ways to induce a [____] ...		
To swap the direction of the [____] [____] ...	or	or
To increase the size of the induced [____] ...	or	

An induced current ....
An induced current ....

....

Microphones

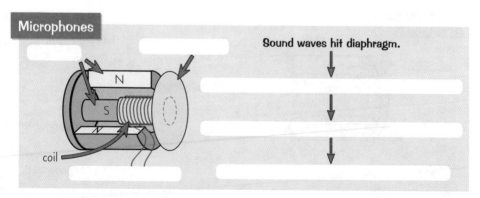

Sound waves hit diaphragm.

coil

Generators and Transformers

Alternators

Alternators generate _____ _____ .

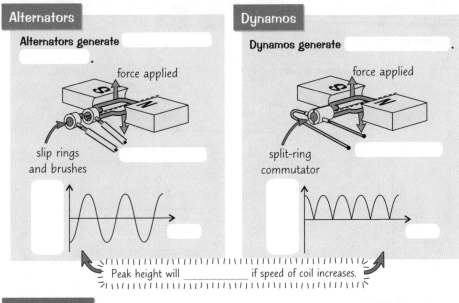

force applied

slip rings
and brushes

Dynamos

Dynamos generate _____ .

force applied

split-ring
commutator

Peak height will _____ if speed of coil increases.

Transformers

_____ passed through
primary coil.

Changing _____ induced in
iron core.

_____ induced in
secondary coil.

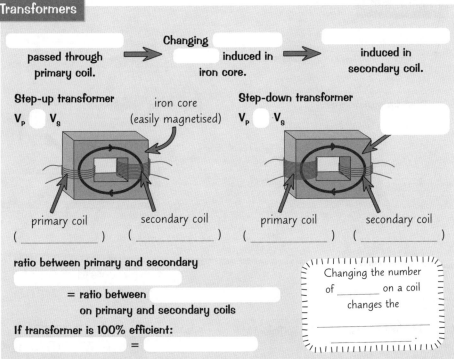

Step-up transformer
V_P ___ V_S

iron core
(easily magnetised)

primary coil   secondary coil
(_____)   (_____)

Step-down transformer
V_P ___ V_S

primary coil   secondary coil
(_____)   (_____)

ratio between primary and secondary

_____

= ratio between _____
on primary and secondary coils

If transformer is 100% efficient:

_____ = _____

Changing the number
of _____ on a coil
changes the
_____
_____ .

 ✓   ✓   ✓

Topic 7 — Magnetism and Electromagnetism

Generators and Transformers

Alternators

Alternators generate [_____]
[_____].

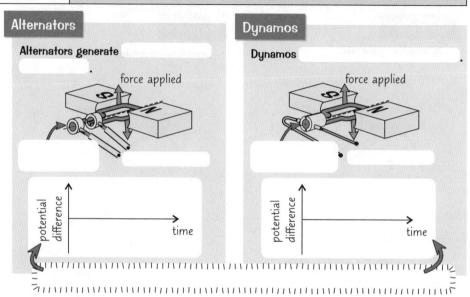

force applied

Dynamos

Dynamos [_____].

force applied

Transformers

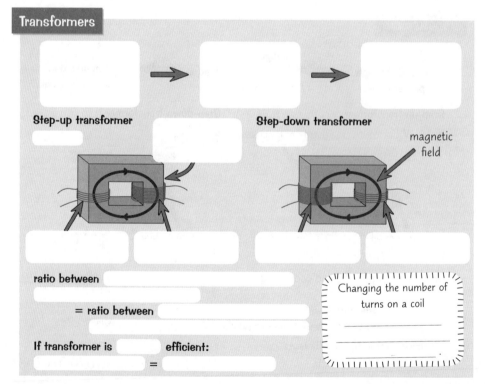

Step-up transformer

Step-down transformer

magnetic field

ratio between [_____]

[_____] = ratio between [_____]
[_____]

If transformer is [_____] efficient:
[_____] = [_____]

Changing the number of turns on a coil

....

....

....

Topic 7 — Magnetism and Electromagnetism

Mixed Practice Quizzes

Keep that motor turning, it's time for some quick quiz questions on pages 121-130.
Time to see if you can transform your revision into the correct answers...

Quiz 1   Date: ...... / ...... / ......

1) True or false? A compass needle points in
   the direction of the magnetic field it's in.

2) What is an electromagnet?

3) Name two magnetic materials.

4) Where is the magnetic field of a bar magnet strongest?

5) Describe the motor effect.

6) In Fleming's left-hand rule, which digit shows the direction of the current?

7) What type of generator produces direct current?

8) What is a permanent magnet?

9) What type of transformer has a higher potential difference
   across its secondary coil than across its primary coil?

10) Give one way to reverse the direction of an induced potential
    difference that was caused by moving a wire inside a magnetic field.

Total:

Quiz 2   Date: ...... / ...... / ......

1) Describe the force between two magnets when
   their south poles are brought close to each other.

2) Which coil has more turns in a step-down transformer?

3) What is a magnetic field?

4) In Fleming's left-hand rule, what does the thumb show the direction of?

5) True or false? A cobalt rod cannot become an induced magnet.

6) What is a solenoid with an iron core called?

7) Describe how a simple electric motor works.

8) How can you increase the size of an induced potential difference?

9) What is the generator effect?

10) Describe the magnetic field shape around a straight current-carrying wire.

Total:

Topic 7 — Magnetism and Electromagnetism

Mixed Practice Quizzes

Quiz 3   Date: ...... / ...... / ......

1) What two factors affect the magnetic field strength around a current-carrying wire?

2) What type of current is generated by a dynamo?

3) How does magnetic field strength change with distance from a magnet?

4) True or false? Magnetic forces are contact forces.

5) Describe the magnetic field inside a solenoid.

6) How will the force on a wire due to the motor effect change if the current through it is increased?

7) True or false? An induced current will generate a magnetic field that opposes the change that made it.

8) Describe how a simple transformer works.

9) Why does a compass needle point north when it's not near a magnet?

10) Describe how loudspeakers produce sound waves from alternating current.

Total:

Quiz 4   Date: ...... / ...... / ......

1) True or false? Moving a magnet in and out of a coil of wire will induce a potential difference across the coil.

2) What does the direction of magnetic field lines show?

3) What device converts sound waves into alternating current?

4) For what kind of transformer is $V_p > V_s$ true?

5) Which pole do magnetic field lines point towards?

6) What happens to the magnetic field of an induced magnet when it is removed from an external magnetic field?

7) How does adding an iron core to a solenoid affect its magnetic field?

8) In Fleming's left-hand rule, which digit shows the direction of the magnetic field?

9) What three things affect the size of the force caused by the motor effect?

10) True or false? The magnetic field outside a solenoid is strong and uniform.

Total:

Stars and the Solar System

The Life Cycle of a Star

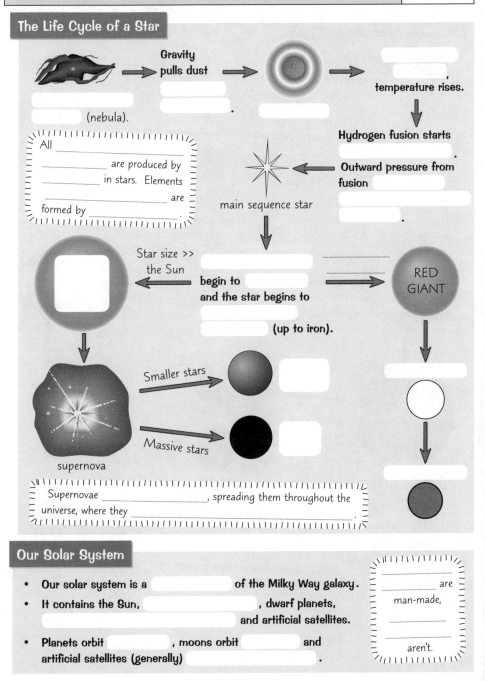

Gravity pulls dust

_____ (nebula).

_____ . temperature rises.

Hydrogen fusion starts
_____ .

Outward pressure from fusion
_____ .

main sequence star

All _____ are produced by _____ in stars. Elements _____ are formed by _____

Star size >> the Sun

begin to _____ and the star begins to _____ (up to iron).

RED GIANT

Smaller stars

Massive stars

supernova

Supernovae _____, spreading them throughout the universe, where they _____ .

Our Solar System

- Our solar system is a _____ of the Milky Way galaxy.
- It contains the Sun, _____, dwarf planets, _____ and artificial satellites.
- Planets orbit _____, moons orbit _____ and artificial satellites (generally) _____ .

_____ are man-made, _____ aren't.

Stars and the Solar System

The Life Cycle of a Star

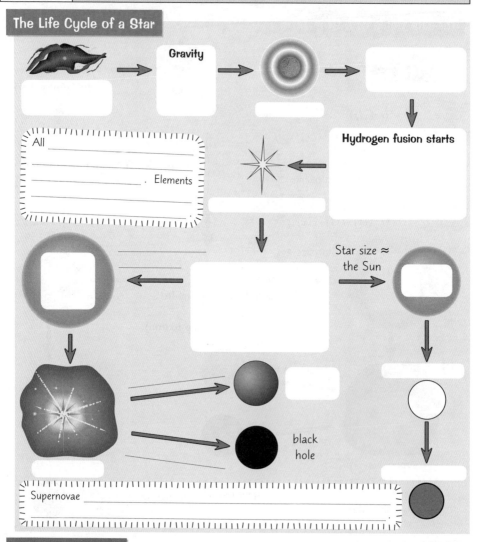

Gravity

Hydrogen fusion starts

All _____ _____ _____ . Elements

Star size ≈ the Sun

black hole

Supernovae _____ _____ _____

Our Solar System

- Our solar system is a tiny part of the

- It contains

- Planets orbit

 ✓ ✓ ✓

Orbits, Red-Shift and The Big Bang

First Go:
..... /..... /.....

Circular Orbits

Gravitational force keeps

and _____ in _____

_____.

It causes the object's _____ to _____ _____.

This means the object's _____

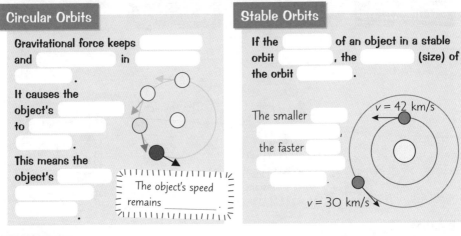

The object's speed remains _____.

Stable Orbits

If the _____ of an object in a stable orbit _____, the _____ (size) of the orbit _____.

The smaller _____,

the faster _____

$v = 42$ km/s

$v = 30$ km/s

Red-Shift

RED-SHIFT — an _____ in the _____ of light (light is shifted towards the _____ of the spectrum). Observed when a _____ from the Earth.

The _____ observed from _____ is _____.

The further away the galaxy:

• the _____ it _____

• the _____ its _____

_____

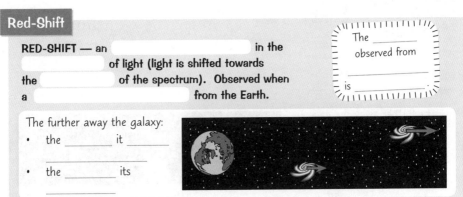

The Big Bang Theory and Universal Mysteries

Big Bang theory:

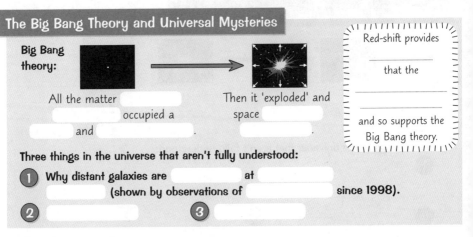

All the matter _____ occupied a _____ and _____

Then it 'exploded' and space _____.

Red-shift provides _____ that the _____ _____ and so supports the Big Bang theory.

Three things in the universe that aren't fully understood:

① Why distant galaxies are _____ at _____ _____ (shown by observations of _____ since 1998).

② _____

③ _____

 ☑ ☑ ☑

Topic 8 — Space Physics

Orbits, Red-Shift and The Big Bang

Circular Orbits

Gravitational force

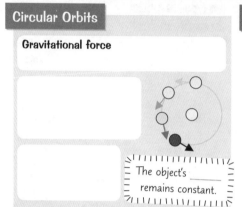

The object's .... remains constant.

Stable Orbits

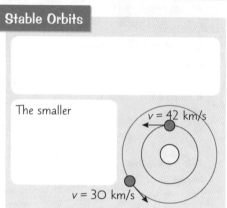

The smaller

$v = 42$ km/s

$v = 30$ km/s

Red-Shift

RED-SHIFT —

The ....

The further away the galaxy:
- ....
- ....

The Big Bang Theory and Universal Mysteries

Big Bang theory:

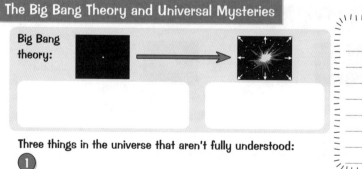

Three things in the universe that aren't fully understood:

1

2   3

Red-shift

Mixed Practice Quizzes

Reinforce your universal knowledge by answering questions on p.133-136 below.

Quiz 1   Date: ...... / ...... / ......

1) True or false? Faster planets in stable orbits have larger orbital radii than slower planets in stable orbits.

2) What is red-shift?

3) How is the distance of a galaxy related to the amount of red-shift it has?

4) Which galaxy is our solar system in?

5) What type of star comes between a nebula and a main sequence star in a star's life cycle?

6) Describe the life cycle of a star that is the same size as the Sun.

7) True or false? Moons orbit planets.

8) How does a protostar become a main sequence star?

9) What do observations of supernovae since 1998 show that scientists cannot yet explain?

10) What force keeps planets and satellites in circular orbits?

Total:

Quiz 2   Date: ...... / ...... / ......

1) True or false? The Sun will become a neutron star in the future.

2) Two planets, travelling in stable orbits at different speeds, orbit around the same star. Will they have the same or different orbital radii?

3) Describe how a galaxy's distance from Earth is related to its speed.

4) True or false? Dark matter isn't fully understood by scientists.

5) What determines whether a star becomes a red giant or a red super giant?

6) Which stage of a star's life cycle creates elements heavier than iron?

7) Describe how the Sun was formed.

8) Which property — direction, velocity or speed — remains constant for an object in a circular orbit?

9) Give one example of a natural satellite.

10) What evidence does red-shift provide that supports the Big Bang theory?

Total:

Mixed Practice Quizzes

Quiz 3 Date: ...... / ...... / ......

1) Describe how the universe began, according to the Big Bang theory.
2) Name both possible stages of a star's life cycle after a supernova.
3) What is a nebula?
4) Observations of what objects show that distant galaxies are receding at increasing speeds?
5) What balances the inward force of gravity in a main sequence star?
6) How many planets orbit the Sun?
7) Which move away from us faster — closer galaxies or distant galaxies?
8) State two properties that constantly change for a satellite in a circular orbit.
9) Describe how elements produced in stars more massive than the Sun are distributed throughout the universe.
10) True or false? Red-shift is an observed decrease in the wavelength of light.

Total:

Quiz 4 Date: ...... / ...... / ......

1) Does a galaxy have to be moving towards or away from the Earth for us to observe a red-shift from it?
2) Describe the initial state of all the matter in the universe, according to the Big Bang theory.
3) True or false? The Sun is a star in our solar system.
4) Describe the life cycle of a star that is much larger than the Sun.
5) What happens to the radius of a planet's orbit if the speed of the planet decreases but the orbit remains stable?
6) What do a) moons orbit? b) planets orbit?
7) Give one example of something in the universe that isn't fully understood by scientists.
8) Is red-shift an observed increase or decrease in the wavelength of light?
9) What process in stars produces all naturally occurring elements?
10) True or false? Electrostatic forces keep artificial satellites in circular orbits.

Total:

Required Practicals 1

Specific Heat Capacity

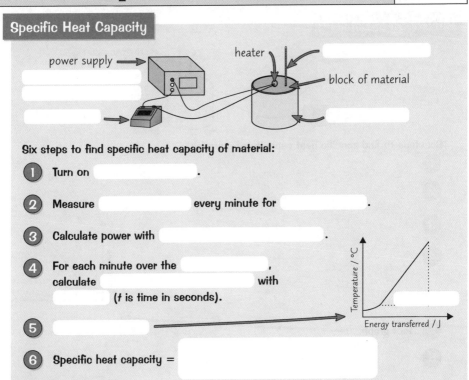

power supply →

heater

block of material

Six steps to find specific heat capacity of material:

1. Turn on _____ .

2. Measure _____ every minute for _____ .

3. Calculate power with _____ .

4. For each minute over the _____ , calculate _____ with _____ (t is time in seconds).

5. _____ →

6. Specific heat capacity = _____

Temperature / °C

Energy transferred / J

Thermal Insulators

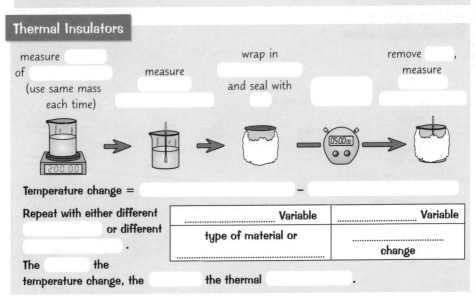

measure _____ of (use same mass each time)

measure _____

wrap in _____ and seal with _____

remove _____ , measure _____

Temperature change = _____ — _____

Repeat with either different _____ or different _____ .

.... Variable	.... Variable
type of material or	.... change

The _____ the temperature change, the _____ the thermal _____ .

Required Practicals 1

Specific Heat Capacity

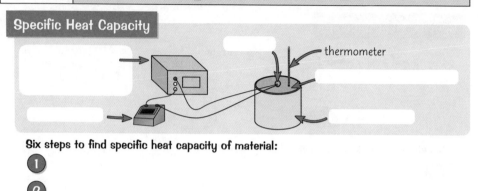

thermometer

Six steps to find specific heat capacity of material:

1

2

3

4

5 Plot graph.

6

Thermal Insulators

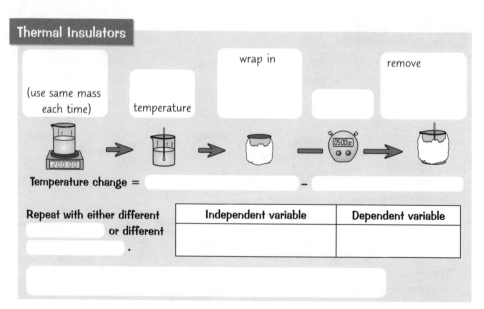

(use same mass each time)

temperature

wrap in

remove

Temperature change =   −

Repeat with either different
_____ or different
_____ .

Independent variable	Dependent variable

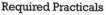

Required Practicals 2

Two Resistance Experiments

1️⃣ Changing _____ (at a _____).

• Change length of wire by moving _____.

• For each length, _____ with _____.

Independent Variable	
Dependent Variable	

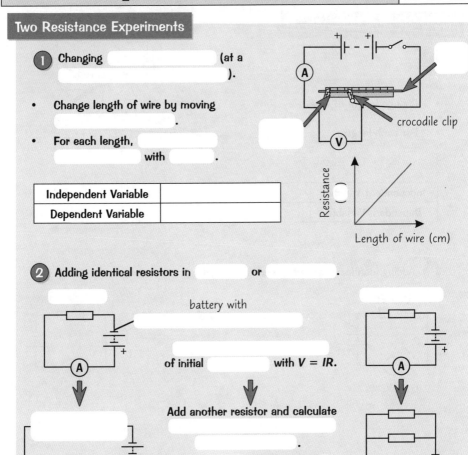

crocodile clip

Resistance ( ) / Length of wire (cm)

2️⃣ Adding identical resistors in _____ or _____ .

battery with _____

of initial _____ with $V = IR$.

Add another resistor and calculate _____.

_____ until at least _____ have been added in total.

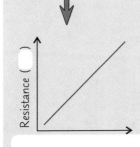

Resistance ( )

Independent Variable	
Dependent Variable	resistance

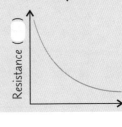

Resistance ( )

Required Practicals 2

Two Resistance Experiments

1

- Change length of wire

- For each length,

metre ruler

Independent Variable	
Dependent Variable	

2 Adding identical resistors in series or parallel

SERIES

Independent Variable	
Dependent Variable	

Required Practicals

Required Practicals 3

I-V Characteristics

Three steps to find a component's *I-V* characteristic:

1 Vary [____] to change [____] through circuit, and then take a reading of [____].
[____].

2 [____] connected to battery (so current is [____]) and repeat [____].

3 Plot values on [____].

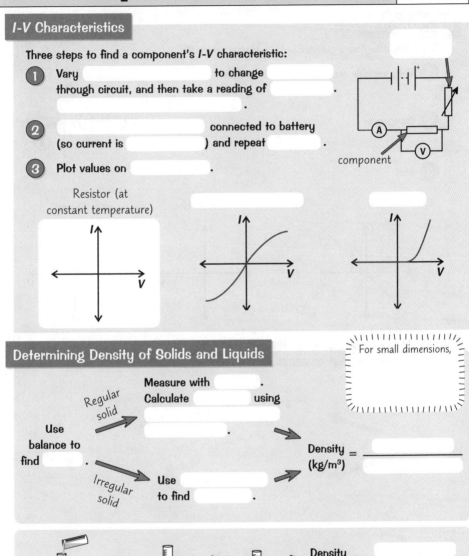

Resistor (at constant temperature)

Determining Density of Solids and Liquids

For small dimensions,

Regular solid

Measure with [____].
Calculate [____] using [____].

Use balance to find [____].

Irregular solid

Use [____] to find [____].

Density = [____]
(kg/m³)

Pour [____] of [____] into [____] on balance.

Record [____] and [____].

[____] this until [____].

Density = [____]
(kg/m³)

Use the [____] for each measurement. Then take an [____] of calculated [____].

Required Practicals 3

I-V Characteristics

Three steps to find a component's I-V characteristic:

variable resistor

1 **Vary variable resistor**

2 **Swap over**

3 **Plot**

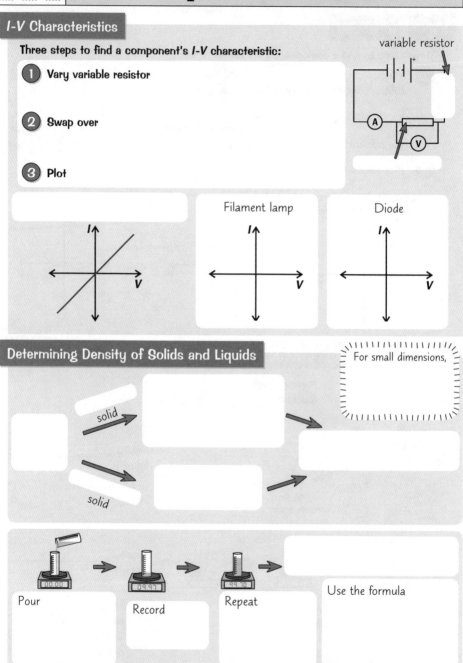

| | Filament lamp | Diode |

Determining Density of Solids and Liquids

For small dimensions,

solid

solid

Pour

Record

Repeat

Use the formula

Required Practicals 4

Investigating Springs

Four steps to find the relationship between force and extension:

1. Measure [_____] of [_____] with [_____].

2. Add [_____] to spring (causing it to [_____]).

3. Calculate force and extension:

    Force = ... = ...
    (....... is .... on spring, ... is
    ....)

    Extension = ...

4. Add [_____] and calculate new [_____] and [_____]. Repeat for at least [_____].

Independent Variable	
Dependent Variable	

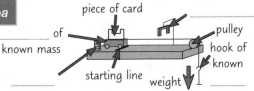
fixed ruler
hanging mass

Force (N) vs Extension (m) graph

Two Experiments that Test F = ma

piece of card
.... of known mass
pulley
hook of known [_____]
starting line
weight

1. Increase mass

- Add [_____].
- Release [_____] from [_____].
  [_____] records trolley's acceleration.
- Add [_____] to trolley and repeat until [_____].

Independent Variable	
Dependent Variable	acceleration
Control Variable	

Increasing [_____]
[_____] acceleration.

2. Increase force

- Start with [_____].
- Move one to [_____] and [_____] trolley from [_____]. Light gate records trolley's [_____].
- Move another [_____] and repeat until all masses [_____].

Independent Variable	Dependent Variable	Control Variable
	acceleration	

Increasing [_____] increases acceleration.

Required Practicals 4

Investigating Springs

Four steps to find the relationship between force and extension:

1 Measure

2 Add mass

3 Calculate force and extension:

4 Add another mass

Independent Variable	
Dependent Variable	

Extension (m)

Two Experiments that Test $F = ma$

1 Increase

- Add mass
- Release trolley

- Add another mass

Independent Variable	
Dependent Variable	
Control Variable	

Increasing

pulley

hook of known mass

starting line

2 Increase

- Start with
- Move one

- Move another

Independent Variable	Dependent Variable	Control Variable

Increasing

Required Practicals 5

Two Ways to Measure Wave Speed

1 Waves in a ripple tank.

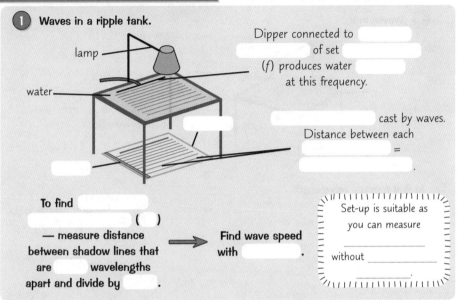

lamp

water

Dipper connected to [_____]
[_____] of set
(*f*) produces water [_____]
at this frequency.

[_____] cast by waves.
Distance between each
[_____] =
[_____].

To find [_____]
[_____] ( )
— measure distance
between shadow lines that
are [_____] wavelengths
apart and divide by [_____].

→ **Find wave speed
with** [_____].

Set-up is suitable as
you can measure
....
without ....
....

2 Waves in a solid.

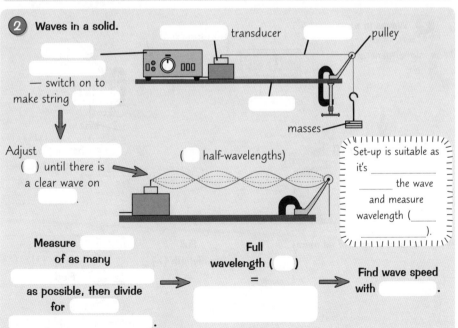

[_____] transducer [_____] pulley

[_____]
— switch on to
make string [_____].

↓

Adjust [_____]
( ) until there is
a clear wave on
[_____].

(half-wavelengths)

masses

Set-up is suitable as
it's ....
.... the wave
and measure
wavelength (_____
........................).

Measure [_____]
of as many
[_____]
as possible, then divide
for [_____].

→ **Full
wavelength ( )**
=
[_____]

→ **Find wave speed
with** [_____].

 ✓ ✓ ☺ ✓

Required Practicals 5

Two Ways to Measure Wave Speed

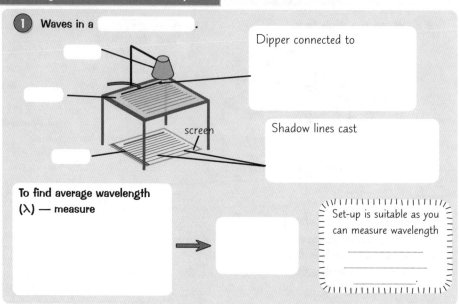

1 Waves in a [_____].

Dipper connected to [_____]

[_____]

[_____]

[_____]

screen

Shadow lines cast [_____]

To find average wavelength (λ) — measure

[_____] → [_____]

Set-up is suitable as you can measure wavelength
....
....
....

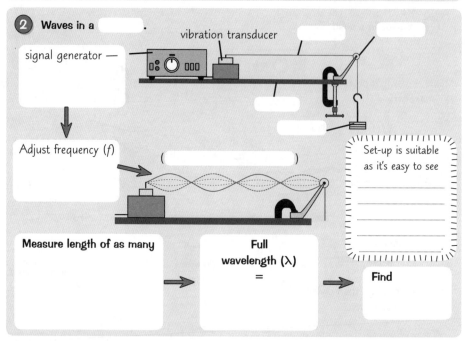

2 Waves in a [_____].

vibration transducer

[_____]

signal generator — [_____]

[_____]

Adjust frequency (f)

([_____])

Set-up is suitable as it's easy to see
....
....
....
....
....

Measure length of as many [_____] →

Full wavelength (λ) = [_____] →

Find [_____]

 ✓ ✓ ✓

Required Practicals 6

Refraction and Reflection

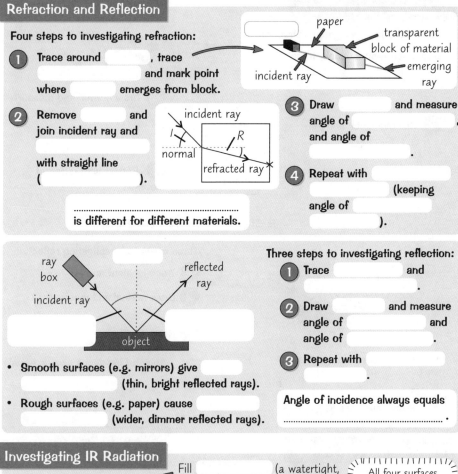

Four steps to investigating refraction:

1. Trace around [____], trace [_____] and mark point where [____] emerges from block.

paper

transparent block of material

incident ray

emerging ray

2. Remove [____] and join incident ray and [_____] with straight line ([_____]).

incident ray

I

R

normal

refracted ray

3. Draw [____] and measure angle of [_____], and angle of [_____].

4. Repeat with [_____] (keeping angle of [_____]).

.... is different for different materials.

ray box

reflected ray

incident ray

object

Three steps to investigating reflection:

1. Trace [_____] and [_____].

2. Draw [____] and measure angle of [_____] and angle of [_____].

3. Repeat with [_____].

- Smooth surfaces (e.g. mirrors) give [_____] (thin, bright reflected rays).

- Rough surfaces (e.g. paper) cause [_____] (wider, dimmer reflected rays).

Angle of incidence always equals ....

Investigating IR Radiation

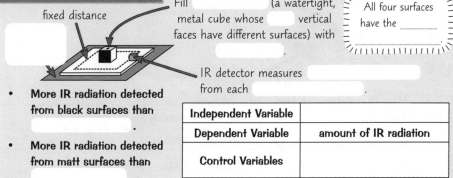

fixed distance

Fill [_____] (a watertight, metal cube whose [____] vertical faces have different surfaces) with [_____].

All four surfaces have the ....

IR detector measures [_____] from each [_____].

- More IR radiation detected from black surfaces than [_____].

- More IR radiation detected from matt surfaces than [_____].

Independent Variable	
Dependent Variable	amount of IR radiation
Control Variables	

Required Practicals

Required Practicals 6

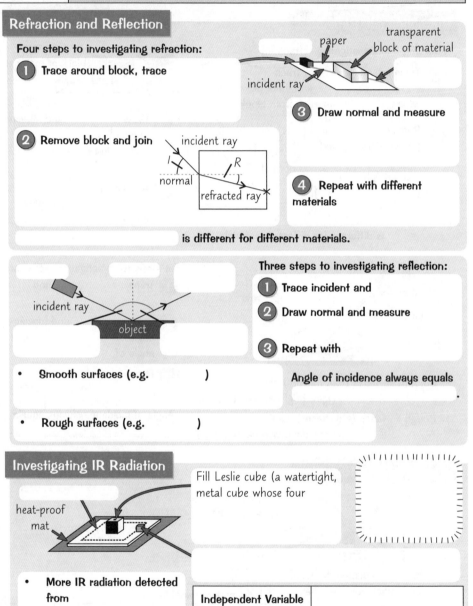

Refraction and Reflection

Four steps to investigating refraction:

1. Trace around block, trace

paper — transparent block of material

incident ray

2. Remove block and join

incident ray

I

normal

R

refracted ray

3. Draw normal and measure

4. Repeat with different materials

_____ is different for different materials.

Three steps to investigating reflection:

incident ray

object

1. Trace incident and

2. Draw normal and measure

3. Repeat with

• Smooth surfaces (e.g.   )

• Rough surfaces (e.g.   )

Angle of incidence always equals _____ .

Investigating IR Radiation

heat-proof mat

Fill Leslie cube (a watertight, metal cube whose four

• More IR radiation detected from

• More IR radiation detected from

Independent Variable	
Dependent Variable	
Control Variables	

 ✓ ✓ ✓

Mixed Practice Quizzes

Phew, what a lot of practicals. Here are some quizzes for you testing p.139-150.

Quiz 1   Date: ...... / ...... / ......

1) Describe how to find the specific heat capacity of a material.
2) What shape is the *I-V* graph for a filament lamp?
3) List the apparatus needed for the trolley experiment that tests $F = ma$.
4) How can you measure the volume of an irregular solid?
5) What is the dependent variable in an experiment that tests the thermal insulation of different materials?
6) How do you find the average wavelength of water waves in a ripple tank?
7) In the trolley experiment that tests $F = ma$, what provides the force?
8) Name one piece of apparatus that can be used to provide a beam of light.
9) True or false? All the surfaces of a Leslie cube have different temperatures.
10) Describe how to set up an experiment to investigate how the resistance of a wire changes with length.

Total:

Quiz 2   Date: ...... / ...... / ......

1) How can you use a graph of temperature against energy transferred (from the specific heat capacity experiment) to calculate specific heat capacity?
2) How does the resistance of a wire vary with its length?
3) Describe an experiment you could perform to compare the effectiveness of different materials as thermal insulators.
4) Name two pieces of apparatus used for measuring small dimensions.
5) What piece of apparatus can be used to measure a trolley's acceleration?
6) Describe how to determine the density of a liquid.
7) How do you calculate the force acting on a spring with hanging masses?
8) What is a Leslie cube?
9) Describe an experiment you could do to investigate the amount of IR radiation emitted from different surfaces.
10) Describe an experiment to measure the wave speed on a piece of string.

Total:

Mixed Practice Quizzes

Quiz 3 — Date: ...... / ...... / ......

1) In an experiment investigating the relationship between the length of a wire and its resistance, what would the independent variable be?

2) Describe an experiment you could do to investigate how the resistance in a circuit is affected by adding identical resistors in series.

3) Give one possible independent variable in the thermal insulators experiment.

4) How can you determine the density of a regular solid?

5) How do you calculate the extension of a spring from its natural length?

6) When using a trolley to test how increasing the force applied affects acceleration, what is the control variable?

7) Why is the experimental set-up for measuring the wavelength of water waves in a ripple tank suitable?

8) Describe an experiment you could do to investigate refraction.

9) Name a piece of safety apparatus that should be used with a Leslie cube.

10) Describe the experimental set-up to find a material's specific heat capacity.

Total:

Quiz 4 — Date: ...... / ...... / ......

1) How do you calculate the temperature change of a liquid that is cooling down from its initial temperature and final temperature?

2) Give the independent variable in an experiment that investigates how the total resistance of a circuit changes when adding resistors in parallel.

3) Describe an experiment to find a component's *I-V* characteristic.

4) List the apparatus needed in an experiment to find the density of a liquid.

5) Describe two experiments you can do to test $F = ma$.

6) Describe how to measure the speed of water waves in a ripple tank.

7) List the apparatus needed in an experiment that investigates refraction.

8) Describe an experiment you could do to investigate reflection of light.

9) Name an electrical component used to vary the current through a circuit.

10) Describe an experiment to find the force-extension relationship of a spring.

Total:

Apparatus and Techniques

Measuring Length

ruler should be

to object

can measure small distances accurately.

use a
to make sure you always

take reading at

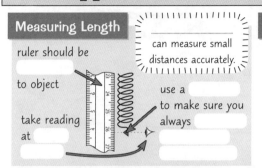

Measuring Angles

align angle vertex with

measure the angle

line up

with one angle line

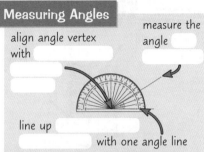

Measuring the Volume of a Liquid

(draws up liquid)

transfers accurate

graduated

pick suitable size for

read from

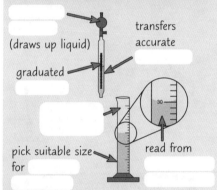

Measuring the Volume of a Solid

fill
with water to just

put the object in and

in a measuring cylinder

object's volume =

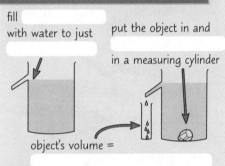

Measuring Temperature

wait for

to stabilise

bulb fully

read off scale at

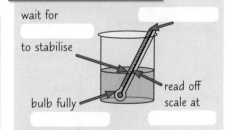

Safety

safety

If using _____, don't look
.

follow

use clamp stands to stop

gloves

handle

with care

don't touch

(e.g. closed shoes)

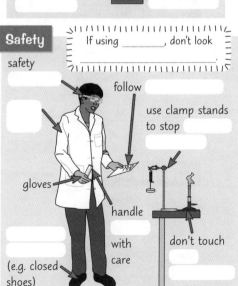

Measuring Mass

liquid or solid to

balance
(
)

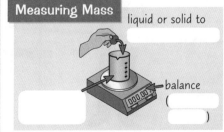

Apparatus and Techniques

Measuring Length

ruler should be

Micrometers

use a

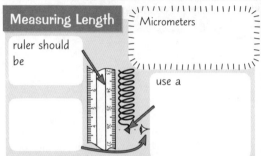

Measuring Angles

align angle

measure

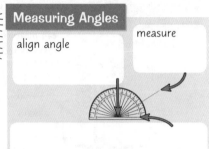

Measuring the Volume of a Liquid

transfers

graduated pipette

pick suitable

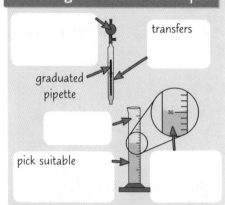

Measuring the Volume of a Solid

put the object in and

Measuring Temperature

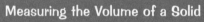

wait for

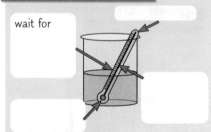

Safety

If using _____

_____ .

use

handle

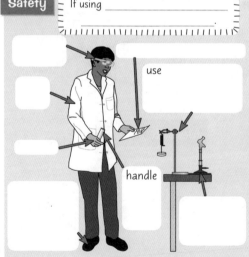

Measuring Mass

liquid

empty container

Working with Electronics

Voltmeters

Connect a voltmeter [_____] with a device to measure the [_____] across it.

Ammeters

Connect an ammeter [_____] with a device to measure the current [_____].

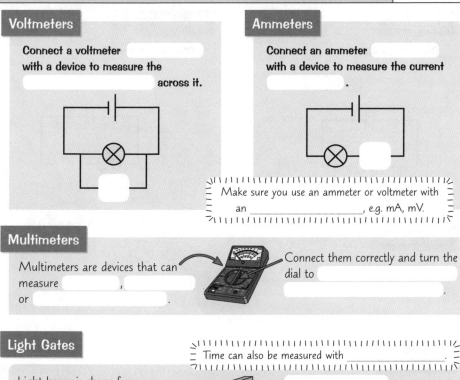

Make sure you use an ammeter or voltmeter with an _____, e.g. mA, mV.

Multimeters

Multimeters are devices that can measure [_____], [_____] or [_____].

Connect them correctly and turn the dial to [_____].

Light Gates

Time can also be measured with _____.

Light beam is shone from [_____] to [_____].

[_____] to computer.
Computer measures time that light beam is [_____].

Two quantities measured using light gates:

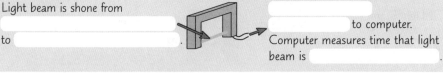

1 **Speed**

Use [_____] and time that light beam is broken to [_____].

object passes through [_____]

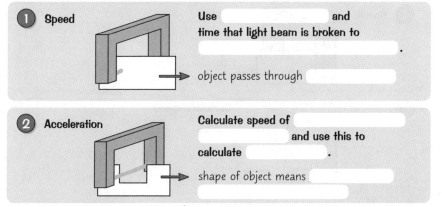

2 **Acceleration**

Calculate speed of [_____] [_____] and use this to calculate [_____].

shape of object means [_____]

Second Go:
...../...../.....

Working with Electronics

Voltmeters

Connect a voltmeter

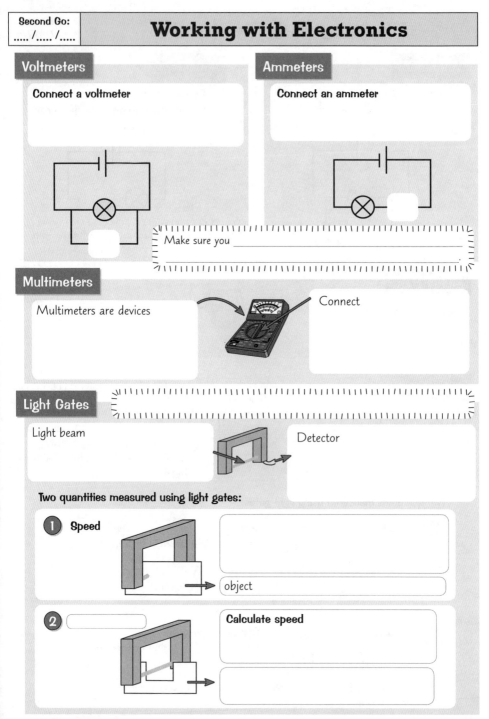

Ammeters

Connect an ammeter

Make sure you ....

Multimeters

Multimeters are devices

Connect

Light Gates

Light beam

Detector

Two quantities measured using light gates:

1 **Speed**

object

2 ....

Calculate speed

Mixed Practice Quizzes

Final question time, don't be too sad. These delightful quiz questions test the content from pages 153-156. You know the drill by now — get cracking.

Quiz 1   Date: ...... / ...... / ......

1) True or false? An ammeter should always be connected in parallel with the device it is measuring.

2) What does a pipette filler do?

3) What is a multimeter?

4) Where should the water be filled to in a eureka can, before an object is put in?

5) Give two quantities that can be measured using a light gate.

6) Why should a clamp stand be used when suspending masses from a spring?

7) What is a measuring cylinder used for?

8) Give two things you must do when measuring the length of an object.

9) Name the apparatus used for measuring the angle between two lines.

10) What value should a mass balance be set to before measuring mass?

Total:

Quiz 2   Date: ...... / ...... / ......

1) Give one safety precaution you should follow when working with lasers.

2) How does a light gate work?

3) True or false? You should take a thermometer reading at eye level.

4) When measuring the length of an object, what could a marker be used for?

5) Give two ways of measuring the volume of a liquid.

6) True or false? A voltmeter should always be connected in parallel with the device to be measured.

7) What is a eureka can used for?

8) An object passes through a light gate. What two quantities are needed to calculate the speed of the object?

9) How should you use a protractor to measure an angle?

10) What apparatus can be used to accurately measure very small distances?

Total:

Practical Skills

Mixed Practice Quizzes

Quiz 3

Date: ...... / ...... / ......

1) What device is capable of measuring either current or potential difference?
2) What is a protractor used for?
3) Give two pieces of apparatus that can measure time.
4) When used correctly, what is the volume of water collected from a eureka can equal to?
5) Which part of a protractor should you align the angle vertex with?
6) What is a light gate connected to?
7) What apparatus could you use to transfer an accurate volume of liquid?
8) Give four possible safety precautions you could take during an experiment.
9) How should you connect an ammeter to measure the current of a device?
10) Describe how to use a light gate to measure the acceleration of an object.

Total:

Quiz 4

Date: ...... / ...... / ......

1) True or false? You should measure the temperature reading on a thermometer as soon as the bulb is fully submerged in a liquid.
2) How is a eureka can used to measure the volume of an irregular solid?
3) What is a graduated pipette used for?
4) What is a micrometer used for?
5) Which part of the meniscus should readings be taken from when measuring volume?
6) How should you connect a voltmeter to measure the voltage of a device?
7) How many times does an object need to interrupt the light beam of a light gate to measure its acceleration?
8) When using a ruler, what can you use to make sure you always measure length from the same point?
9) Name three safety items that can be worn whilst performing an experiment.
10) True or false? A ruler should be perpendicular to an object when measuring its length.

Total:

PANR41